MUSIC OF THE ITALIAN RENAISSANCE

Da Capo Press Music Reprint Series

GENERAL EDITOR

FREDERICK FREEDMAN

Vassar College

MUSIC OF THE ITALIAN RENAISSANCE

By NESTA DE ROBECK

With a New Preface by the Author

DA CAPO PRESS • NEW YORK • 1969

A Da Capo Press Reprint Edition

First Da Capo Printing – August 1969
Second Da Capo Printing – May 1971

This Da Capo Press edition of Nesta De Robeck's *Music of the Italian Renaissance* is an unabridged republication of the first edition published in 1928 by The Medici Society, London. It is reprinted by special arrangement with the original publisher.

Library of Congress Catalog Card Number 69-12689
306-71232-6

A Division of Plenum Publishing Corporation
227 West 17th Street
New York, N.Y. 10011

Printed in the United States of America

PREFACE

THIS book was written many years ago because, like those who see the great buildings of Florence, who see pictures of people playing a variety of instruments and of others obviously singing, I wanted to have an idea of what music had meant to them. Let me say at once that the longer one's interest lasts the more there is to learn.

We know that Pietro Casella's songs delighted Dante; and thanks to the researches of the late Doctor Robert Davidsohn and to those of Professor Fernando Liuzzi we can recapture something of the music in Florence and Umbria in the thirteenth and fourteenth centuries. The later centuries are far better known.

A big disappointment, however, awaits us in the Communal Library of Assisi. It possesses a beautiful early codex of Saint Francis' "Canticle of the Sun" but the lines that should give us the music are empty! Celano tells us how in joyful moments Francis' "Canticle of the Sun," but the lines that should give us voice on a viol represented by a stick. He had been in Florence and though, as elsewhere, only a few could follow his example, the Florentines responded warmly to his personality and in some degree wanted to follow his lead. This outer circle of his Third Order played a considerable part in the life of their city and time. Saint Clare had sent her sister to establish a convent of Poor Ladies and before long the Friars were firmly settled in the church and convent of Santa Croce, while at the other side of the city the Dominicans were established in Santa Maria Novella, which rapidly became a center of studies and art.

Florence was then a city of towers which seemed to be competing in a race to reach the sky; it was a city of splendid buildings and narrow streets into which were crowded something like 100,000 inhabitants. Among these were many prosperous bankers and money-changers and two hundred wool shops; and for genius, energy, and perseverance the Florentines were hard to beat. They could also boast of an adequate legal social system and of what seemed a sufficiency of hospital care. Politics, dominated by the Pope and Emperor, naturally impinged on the city life, but not sufficiently to quell their proud independence of spirit.

The Jubilee of 1300 brought many foreigners through Florence: contacts were established, all useful both to politics and trade. One wonders if they frequented the meetings of the then very popular *laude* singers. It would seem more than likely. Within a relatively short time there had arisen ten different companies of these singers, ordinary citizens who enjoyed meeting together to sing the praise of God and the Madonna.

It required heroism to go off into the desert of the hills like one of the twelve holy men who had left the city to go and lead a life of prayer and penance in the desert of Monte Sennario, but any stay-at-home could join his friends after the day's work to sing together; thus this practice of *laude* singing soon became extremely popular. These singers were attached to the cathedral of Santa Reparata, to the churches of San Lorenzo, Sant' Egidio, San Marco, to the Dominicans of Santa Maria Novella, the Servites of the Santissima Annunziata, the Augustinians of Santo Spirito, the Carmelites of Santa Maria del Carmine, and last but not least those who gathered in Or San Michele. The number speaks for the popularity of *laude* singing. Each company had a leader who was also responsible for looking after the poor and sick, and the company of Or San Michele had an almost official position as a charitable institution. In the church today we see the same picture of Our Lady holding the Child Jesus before which the fourteenth-century *laude* were sung.

The form of these songs varies, but as a rule they consist of three parts: a refrain, a stanza, and the repetition of the refrain. We know them chiefly through the Florence and Cortona manuscripts published by Professor Liuzzi. Some of the Christmas and Easter songs were in Latin; but for the most part Italian was used. This in itself carried the *laude* deep into the lives of the people, while the melodies had something fresh to ears accustomed to the Gregorian chant of the Church.

One *laude* describes paradise with the angels singing songs of love while the holy virgins begin to dance (naturally we think of Fra Angelico in San Marco). Another song urges all present to sing so loudly that the angels will feel bound to answer with a smile. Yet another begs Our Lady to give peace to the Florentines—surely a most heartfelt aspiration.

A further influence in *laude* singing came from the flagellants. These penitential groups arose in many places and what with wars, pestilence, and disasters there was plenty to turn even resilient temperaments toward the Four Last Things or to set them off on pilgrimages to Rome. Their way probably passed through Florence and Umbria. And it was in the country of Saint

Francis that the *laude* form found its most intense expression in the genius of Jacopone da Todi. When he cries "while I draw breath of love I still must sing" was he thinking of a human voice or only of music of the heart?

Artistically the *laudesi* saw to it that their singers and instrumentalists were trained by professors who used as a textbook the *Micrologus* of Guido of Arezzo; and his opinion was that "anyone who makes music without having studied may rightly be called a beast." The volumes published by Professor Liuzzi show what a genuine contribution the songs of the *laudesi* were in the development of our musical heritage. Some of them are for a solo voice, others for solo and chorus, some certainly had an accompaniment: "a good singer needs a good lute player; and if the plucking of the strings follows the voice, the song gains in pleasing."

Indeed a good singer or instrumentalist had a fair chance of a successful career. In Florence, a meeting of the city council in 1333 speaks of ten musicians who were regularly employed "to delight the citizens." Special mention is made of a certain Prezzivalle di Gianni who by his singing gave daily pleasure to many people, for which he was to receive a quarterly gift of "honorable clothing." It was made clear that the gift depended on the artist's punctual observance of the agreement, but if the "honorable clothing" failed to reach the singer when he had earned it, those responsible for the omission were to be punished.

Once a year the various companies indulged in a banquet, and Doctor Davidsohn found details of these feasts in a manuscript in the British Museum. Florentine life was never stagnant: intense artistic, political, commercial, and social activities somehow managed to triumph over wars and feuds. Its good and bad sides are all recorded; also its careful side, thanks to the accurate accounts kept by the Peruzzi family which tell us how much they spent and on what.

There was music and singing in private houses and as we know from the *Decameron* there were songs for all occasions. In the palaces of the rich, in market places, in gardens, and on threshing floors people sang and danced. The fourteenth century needed dance music as surely as it did songs: the instruments that appear in the pictures were never imaginary, but were those in daily use.

In the city and in the country, the Calendimaggio May-day revels were a great occasion for jollification of all kinds, as was also the feast of Saint John the Baptist, the city's patron. But Florentine entertaining of the leisured class comes best to life in the accounts of parties in the villa del Paradiso, outside the Porta San Niccolo. It belonged to the rich Alberti family whose hospitality was evidently lavish and varied. Conjurors and clowns as well as the best musicians of Florence, including the famous Francesco Landino, were there to amuse the guests. When a young lady was invited to sing or dance, good manners required that she should do so without any fuss, keeping her eyes cast down and turning toward the most important person present. Before and after the music, there was animated talk and discussion: the Paradiso was a meeting place in the humane Italian tradition; the precursor of so many hospitable Italian villas. If we had been lucky enough to be invited we should in all likelihood have met the Englishman who flaunts his Garter in the fresco of Santa Maria Novella, or even Chaucer — precursors of so long a list of northern guests.

What riches and variety there is in the records of the Italian cities! It is life-enhancing to come into contact with this down-to-earth humanity just because it has coexisted with the heights of spiritual, artistic, and intellectual attainments. We enjoy it and are grateful that it should be so.

Nesta de Robeck

August 1968

MUSIC OF THE ITALIAN RENAISSANCE

MUSIC OF THE ITALIAN RENAISSANCE

BY

NESTA DE ROBECK

LONDON

THE MEDICI SOCIETY

1928

PRINTED IN ENGLAND
AT THE CURWEN PRESS · PLAISTOW

CONTENTS

MUSIC OF THE ITALIAN RENAISSANCE

I

THE ARS NOVA IN FLORENCE

That vulgar and tavern musick which makes one man merry, another mad, strikes in me a fit of deep devotion.

THIS study is not intended for historians of music, who will find in it nothing new, and much that is important passed over lightly—it is rather in the nature of a guide-book for the amateur, who, like myself, may perhaps be conscious of a lack in many even famous books on the Renaissance.

It is impossible to read, however superficially, about the Renaissance in Italy, to say nothing of looking at Italian pictures, and not realize that music played a great part in the life of that time. Yet how often one searches in vain for any account of it! Mr. Symonds, in his great work on the Renaissance, hardly mentions it; Burckhardt is but little better, and it is almost, if not quite, ignored in countless books dealing with the Courts and Art of Italy. At best it would seem as though Italian music had originated with Palestrina, or the rise of the opera, and all that went before is dismissed with a casual remark or some vague reference.

It is not my object in any way to try to prove that Italian music holds the same place in the Art of the world as Italian painting or sculpture, but between that and almost complete neglect there is a large gap. This it has been my wish in some small way to bridge over for others as interested in the subject as I have been, and who perhaps cannot spend enough time in Italy to do it for themselves.

I have not attempted to enter into all the technical questions involved. For their solution let the reader turn to the great histories of music, where they are admirably dealt with; neither have I tried to give a complete list of the composers of those centuries, for in a work with no musical illustrations long lists of names are apt to be meaningless and dry, and there are first-rate musical dictionaries to supply what I have left out. My idea has been to try to reconstruct something of the relationship of music to the life and other arts of the Renaissance, to realize its particular shade of beauty, and to understand a little of its development. My choice of dates—1300–1600—is purely arbitrary. Music flourished in Italy long before the fourteenth century, and the year 1600 merely represents one of its many turning-points. It is convenient, however, to set oneself a limit, and these centuries have seemed to me in some ways the most neglected.

Most appropriately it is Florence that first commands our attention, and there in the Trecento music was ardently cultivated and considered as indispensable as poetry, or painting, or any other art. Dante could justly boast of Florence as 'la bellissima e famosissima figlia di Roma', and never has her light shone more brightly than it did round about the year 1300.

The Florentine Republic was then the chief political power in Central Italy. The great guilds were organized, trade flourished, education was valued—there was money to spare. Florentine art was starting on its triumphant career with Arnolfo di Cambio, Orcagna, Niccolò and Giovanni Pisano in architecture and sculpture, Taddeo Gaddi, Cimabue, and Giotto in painting. Great palaces were in building; the foundations of Santa Maria Novella and Santa Croce were already laid. Dante's beloved 'Bel San Giovanni' was standing then very much as it is now, and a few years more would see the rise of Giotto's Campanile. The State was served by philosophers such as Brunetto Latini, and the first Italian history was being written by Giovanni Villani. Dante himself was born in 1265, Boccaccio, Cavalcanti, and Sacchetti all about the same time, members of a whole group of poets who were delighting their fellow citizens with the *dolce stil nuovo*. 'Con quanti dolci suon e con che canti io era visitato tutto il giorno', wrote Ser Giovanni, and in music, too, as well as in the other arts, Florence in the Trecento could justly claim a European pre-eminence. Already once before a musical light had shone in Tuscany when Guido di Arezzo, a Benedictine monk in the distant tenth century had founded our modern system of notation. His statue stands to-day in the Piazzo of Arezzo, but a more universal memorial to his genius is in the names of our notes, which have never varied since he took them from a Latin hymn:

Ut queant laxis, *Re*sonare fibris
*Mi*ra gestorum, *Fa*muli tuorum
*Sol*ve polluti *La*bii reatum
*S*ancte *I*ohannes.

In Florence, as elsewhere throughout the Middle Ages, music had been the handmaid of the Church, carefully cultivated in the famous schools of singing established by Pope Gregory the Great, and we have inherited the treasure of Gregorian Plainsong. To that art succeeding centuries could add nothing, for it was a finished, perfect thing, for some people the most sublime expression of musical art. It represented the triumph of the spiritual ideal in music, and its perfection was achieved by the denial of every extraneous element. All instruments except the organ were forbidden in the services of the Church, whose music, like the monastery garden, was shut in on all sides from the outside world. The way to the sky alone was open, and as a language for the soul this music has never been surpassed. It was supreme in its own sphere, but apart from its abstract beauty Plainsong remains also as perfect vocal music. There is all the idea of *bel canto* in the vocalizes of the Graduals, in the singableness of the phrase, the often lovely line of the melody. There is, too, a great dramatic quality, and it must not be forgotten that the Church was also the theatre of medieval society. A volume might well be devoted to the musical aspect of the Liturgical drama and the mystery plays. As each season of the Christian year came round, its underlying dogma and significance was brought before the people in dramatic form—then lives of the saints and local legends were performed, for beside the strict Liturgical drama there were a quantity of most varied dramatic laudi, and what Professor d'Ancona has called 'Sacre Rappresentazioni'. At one time it was the custom to illustrate sermons by acted scenes, and the dramatic genius of the Italian people has always been apparent both in religious and secular art. All these performances had music and singing, and the pure musical beauty and effectiveness of many of the sequences, hymns and other parts, is most striking.

The musical richness of the Church was so great, and so all-embracing that, for several centuries at least, beyond it there was nothing but the casual, spontaneous music which dates from time immemorial, ever since, indeed, there have been spring fields to dance in, and winter evenings to while away, singing round the fire.

The minstrel and the jongleur were among the most popular members of medieval society, for they were welcomed, not only as musicians but as carriers of news and gossip, and castle and cottage door stood ever open to them. They were not encouraged by the ecclesiastical authorities, but side by side with its stately sister of the choir, secular music found its place in Florence as elsewhere, often hindered but never suppressed.

In Tuscany, everything favoured popular music. So much time was spent in the fields and vineyards, so many *feste* took place in the open air, as, indeed, they still do to-day. The Gesù Morto or Corpus Christi processions with their traditional hymns are unchanged, and on the eve of the Nativity of the Blessed Virgin bands of children carry lighted, fantastic lanterns, singing down the country lanes.

The long days of threshing the wheat, or of the vintage, end by songs and dancing on the *aja*, with the pipes, or a stray violin, perhaps, for accompaniment, and how often does one not linger to hear the enchanting *Stornelli* that the peasants sing as they work in the fields! The Italians have always loved singing, and in the thirteenth century their natural inclination was further stimulated by the Franciscan Movement, then in all the novelty of its unique attraction. It seized hold of the people, many of whom joined the Third Order; the friars were their friends, living in their midst, and from the first they encouraged music and singing in a far more general way than the monks had naturally ever thought of doing, and in this sense Mr. Chesterton's remark is quite true, that what Saint Benedict stored Saint Francis scattered. Saint Francis, in his great vision, had heard a 'heavenly melody, intolerably sweet', he had sung and made his companions sing, all through his life, and even at the Porziuncula when he lay dying. Thomas of Celano particularly speaks of the 'New Song' and 'the mellifluous organs and well-modulated voices' of the choir of friars singing for the great ceremony of the canonization, and music was, for a time at least, the chief art of the Franciscan Order. Laud singing soon became immensely popular, and during the thirteenth century nearly every parish had its regular *Compagnia dei Laudesi.* In Florence, the earliest of these societies was founded in 1183, when the *Compagnia dei Laudesi della Beata Virgine Maria* first met in Santa Reparata every Saturday after None, whilst the *Laudesi* of Santa Croce and Or San Michele were still in existence and carrying on their old traditions until late in the eighteenth century. This love of singing coincided most happily with the rise of the lyrical poetry of the *dolce stil nuovo,* and poetry and music were inseparable in the art of the Tuscan poets. Dante, in Paradise, heard the perfect music which is so far above anything produced on earth that 'the sweetest song of this world is but as the noise of a thundercloud when compared to the sounds of the heavenly lyre', and to him it is as much a part of Heaven as the river of light, or the eternal rose. He had always delighted even in the music of earth: 'Dilettosi nel canto ed in ogni suono', and his son Pietro Alighieri complains bitterly that his father's musical compositions had never met with the success they deserved. Many of his ballate and smaller poems were set to music by Casella, 'the grandissimo musico' he greets so affectionately in the *Purgatorio*. Dante begs to hear once again one of those songs that so often in the past had soothed his troubled spirit, and his friend begins the beautiful canzone of the Convitto:

> Amor che nella mente mi ragiona
> Comminciò egli allor si dolcemente
> Che la dolcezza ancor dentro mi suon.

In Trucchi's valuable anthology of Italian poetry we find a quantity of Trecento lyrics with the names of the composers who set them to music, and there is no doubt that Petrarca, Cavalcanti, Sacchetti, Lapo Gianni, Dino Compagni, Folgore di San Gimignano and all their companions were accustomed to hear their verses sung much after the style of the Troubadours and Trouvères. The influence of the minstrels of Provence on early Renaissance poetry has often been recognized; and it was their art which had first fired the imagination of Saint Francis, and their songs must have been well known in Central Italy. As musicians the Troubadours were patient, practical artists, who with infinite trouble had elaborated a most delicate technique by which verses might be set to music without obscuring the metre of the text. The question of rhythm occupied them deeply, and they succeeded in introducing a far more accurate rhythmical notation to that already in use. Their songs were in a sense the meeting-point of sacred and folk music, and from these apparently conflicting elements they built up an art of exquisite grace and refinement. They abounded in fresh ideas, and, above all, they were artists, with not only a brain to understand, but a heart to feel. 'Poco vale il canto che non viene dal cuore', wrote Peirol the Trouvère, and how true his motto was and is! Beside their real worth as poets and musicians, the whole legend and personality of the Troubadours, their lives of adventure and romance, the glamour of the Courts of Love, helped to spread the fame of the Provençal minstrels, and nowhere did they find a warmer welcome than in Tuscany. Florence was a very vital place, and in art as in life the Florentines did nothing gently. They were not particularly interested in theorizing about Art, and were content to leave the puzzling out of rules to the Paduans, who had a taste for such work. To what purpose a treatise on intervals or notation, when there was a new sonnet of Cavalcanti, new rime to be set before the next feast day? Neither foreign nor civil wars lessened their desire for enjoyment, for feasting and display, and the occasion to exercise their quick imagination and shrewd, biting wit.

Dancing, singing, masquerades, and *feste* of every sort followed close one upon another, and as early as 1283 we read of a Company formed in the parish of Santa Felicità to celebrate the feast of Saint John, the patron saint of Florence.

Games and dances filled the day, and the people 'went about the streets led by the "Lord of Love", and feasted together at many banquets'. These were truly the men and women of *The Decameron*, who danced and sang and told stories with the plague raging in their midst, and discussed Art and life under the shadow of death. What more fertile soil than this of Florence could be imagined for the art of the Troubadours? They were acclaimed and imitated on all sides, and there quickly arose a regular group of singers, the *Cantori a libro* and the *Cantori a Liuto*, who followed in the steps of Guillaume de Mâchault and Adam de la Hâle. In the palaces of the nobles, the houses of the bourgeois, or the taverns where the artisans gathered, there the singers were listened to and applauded: and during the intervals of warfare, feud and pestilence, there was the steady ferment of artistic life which never failed to interest this kindly, shrewd, artistic and critical people, who, as surely as the Athenian of old, never wearied of the 'new thing'.

Such conditions were naturally favourable to Art, and we come to the first great landmark of Italian musical history after Plainsong, the *Ars Nova* which made Florence famous throughout Europe.

The *Ars Nova* was no 'new art' of Florentine invention. The name was taken over from Philippe de Vitry, the Bishop of Meaux and author of three works, *Ars Nova*, *Ars Perfecta*, *Liber Musicalium*. He was born in 1290, and as a young intellectual priest probably went with Philippe VI or

Charles IV to the Papal Court at Avignon. There he seems to have known Petrarch, and anyhow had the opportunity of meeting many Italian musicians and thinkers. He was caught by the new ideas of measured music, that great innovation which was finding supporters in every country.

There were Walter Odington and Joannes de Muris in England, the latter a far-sighted historian and critic, who, speaking of the music of his day, said that it contained secrets and possibilities which would astonish later generations. Franko and Garlandia were distinguished theorists and composers in France, and Marchetto di Padova, born in 1271, was, perhaps, with Philippe de Vitry, the most outstanding musical personality of the thirteenth century. All were imbued with the desire for measured music, the necessity for which had arisen with the attempt to combine several vocal parts together, and was also surely partly due to the influence which rhythmical movement and dancing have always had upon music.

Plainsong, where there was only one voice to be considered, could and did have its own individual and beautiful rhythmical structure, based on neither beats nor bars, but on the Arsis and Thesis. It was an elaborate and finished art when the idea of measured music began to dawn, and a system of notation had to be found by which the relative length of the notes could be clearly indicated. Through the tenth and eleventh centuries there had been many attempts at combining two voices, and these compositions were known under the general name of organums, and were often a dreary progression of fourths and fifths. Marchetto di Padova and Philippe de Vitry, on the contrary, really wrote three-part songs that were music, thereby laying the foundation of harmony and counterpoint.

They were the first to introduce a freer use of chromatic intervals, which must have had a most alluring and 'modern' sound to ears unaccustomed to them. They had an instinctive dislike of the interval B–F, and constantly tried to avoid it by adding a B♭ or F♯, thus gradually approaching nearer to our idea of a leading note. It is to these men indirectly that we owe our system of notation, showing the lengths of the notes and of that much discussed thing, the bar. How much that is most beautiful has grown out of it, and yet, time and again, that same idea of the bar, and the consequent heavy beat, has been a trap and bane to composers! The older influence, too, has persisted in many ways most interesting to note. Palestrina avoided the recurring strong beat. Bach, in his instrumental and vocal recitatives, Beethoven in the last quartets, and even Wagner continually escape from it, and to-day our younger composers seem to be reverting or progressing far beyond it. It was a measure of convenience—never an ideal arrangement. Nothing of all this, however, takes away from the genius of men like Marchetto di Padova and Philippe de Vitry, who were pioneers to a whole school of music, and were faced with difficulties which we to-day can hardly even understand.

The Ars Nova in Florence

When the Florentines heard Philippe de Vitry's compositions they were evidently carried away with enthusiasm, and realized that here was the model for which they were seeking. Almost at once a whole group of musicians arose to carry on his work, not in theoretical treatises, but in musical settings of songs which were no sooner composed than they were known and sung all over the town.

We know these musicians through the magnificent manuscript in the Laurentian Library known as the *Squarcialupi Codex*. It had lain, probably untouched, in the library since the days of Giuliano dei Medici, until Professor Bonaventura brought the songs it contains to light again, during the Boccaccio celebrations at Certaldo in 1913. The Manuscript is, in itself, most beautiful. All the poems are written in semi-gothic characters, with the notation in black on six red lines, and each page is illuminated with portraits of the different composers, and an endless variety of ornamentation. There are in all three hundred and forty-nine songs, some tender, some humorous, and they certainly represent very fairly the secular music of Florence during the fourteenth century. The names of the chief composers mentioned in the manuscript are as follows: Giovanni de Cascia, Ghirardellus di Firenze, Jacopo di Bologna, Lorenzo di Firenze, Donato, Monaco Benedettino, Abate Riminese, Niccolo Pontificio, Francesco Landino, Vincenzo Fiorentino.

We know exceedingly little of the individual lives of those composers, often only what is implied in their names. There is a tradition, indeed, that Jacopo di Bologna was stabbed by order of the Duke of Amalfi, whose jealousy he had excited, and Magister Ghirardellus we know to have been very highly thought of as a musician. He set a number of Sacchetti's poems to music and, in one of his sonnets, the poet writes the following words about him: 'Vive, vivendo visse e virtù colse, pochi ci son che faccian tal giornata'. Francesco Landino is, however, the only one about whom any real details are preserved. Villani, who speaks enthusiastically about the whole musical life of Florence, gives a fairly full account of his career, describing him as the leader of a band of musicians, and equally famous both as organist and composer. He was born in 1325, the son of a painter, and quite early in life he became blind; but even in those days, when there can have been very little outside help or facilities in study for anyone without sight, no difficulties turned Landino aside from the path he had chosen. He was soon well known as a musician, and even as a poet; he excelled upon several instruments, but his whole soul seems to have gone into his organ playing, and the Florentines thronged the church to hear 'Il Cieco', who apparently was as beloved as he was admired. His fame spread to Venice, where he spent some time as organist of Saint Mark's, even then renowned for its splendid double organ. The Venetians, indeed, so appreciated Landino's art that whilst in their city he was publicly crowned with laurel; but for us, who can only know Landino the organist from the records of others, it is as a composer that he lives, one might almost say the first European composer of Florence. His work marks a striking out towards new fields, untouched by sacred music and hitherto undreamt of. All his music that has survived is a collection of songs, and, apart from their own charm and originality, they were the models of hundreds of other songs and compositions, which gradually spread and had a quite definite influence upon the subsequent musical art of Europe. Landino died in 1390, and was buried in the Church of San Lorenzo in Florence, where his monument is still to be seen. There he stands, in the familiar dress and cap of a Ghirlandaio Florentine citizen, a small portable organ in his hand, and the serene look of the blind upon his sensitive refined face, while above him two angels play the lute and viole. We cannot now do more than guess at the real scope and importance of the purely instrumental music of Landino and his contemporaries. We only know them from their songs: independent instrumental compositions, if there were any, have been lost, or more probably were never written down, and served merely as improvised preludes to the vocal music. The songs were generally for two or three voices, and the Florentine composers went farther than their predecessors in the subdivision of the value of the notes, thus giving more life and movement to the rhythm, as, for instance, in the delightful *Caccia* of Lorenzo di Firenze. It is even uncertain whether they were originally sung *à cappella* or with an instrumental accompaniment. What is certain is the immediate and overwhelming success which they enjoyed among the people of Florence. Here was music that all could enjoy. The lyrics of Cavalcanti, Sacchetti, Ser Giovanni, and Matteo Frescobaldi were hardly written before they were put to music, and the composers were soon as well known as the authors of the verses themselves. Indeed, Jacopo di Bologna could write:

> Tutti fan di maestri
> Fan madrigali ballate e motetti
> Si è piena la terra di magistroli
> Che loco più non trovan i discepoli.

A contemporary speaks of Landino's songs as 'things from Heaven', and surely music that could excite such feelings in those who heard it is well worth even our attention. Some of these songs were performed a few years ago at the Boccaccio and Dante Centenary celebrations with great success, and they proved to be anything but archaic or merely academic curiosities, as some of us had ignorantly expected. On the contrary, we heard songs that were full of charm, spontaneity and humour, with a touch in them of the Tuscan folk-songs, and we could quite well sympathize with the Florentine public of the Trecento, which greeted them with delight.

The people they did not please were the ecclesiastical authorities, who quite rightly supposed that the time was not far off when the people who had taken so kindly to these new songs would wish to infuse 'fresh life', too, into the music of the Church. Already there were painful signs of such a tendency, and the canons and precentors, who must often have had difficult moments with their more modern-minded organists and choirmasters, were determined that no new methods should interfere with the Plainsong services if they could prevent it. They went so far as to persuade Pope John XXII to issue a Bull expressly forbidding any tampering with the existing chants, and condemning the whole *Ars Nova* as 'having no rest and distorting all Plainsong'. In this they were perfectly right, and we have every cause to be thankful that the music of the Church was preserved untouched. Neither Papal Bull, however, nor any other authority could check the course of secular music, which was now so successfully started, and the *Ars Nova* led to results of which its creators cannot have dreamed.

The Florentine composers were hardly dead before the splendid school of English and Flemish musicians carried the art of counterpoint to a new pinnacle. I know that M. van den Borren, following Tinctoris, ascribes the whole *Ars Nova* to Dunstable, and far be it from me to belittle that great musician. Yet it seems to me that Tinctoris may quite well have overlooked the *Squarcialupi Codex*, for the reputation of Landino and the Trecento Florentines had probably been overshadowed for Tinctoris by the imposing music of the next generation.

Then England in the fourteenth century was a European

power, and there was perpetual intercourse between her and the Continent. Many Englishmen had ties with France, and French and Italian music must have been well known to music lovers in England.

Some of the English sees were filled by foreigners, a perpetual Latin element existed in intellectual circles, and the coming of the friars had opened yet another channel for Continental influences. Florence in the Trecento, thanks to her wealth, her culture, and political genius, had risen to a position equal to that of countries far above her in importance and possessions, and her merchants were in every capital as ambassadors of the Republic and as traders, carrying everywhere the fame of her achievements. When Edward III wanted money for the disastrous Hundred Years' War, he turned to the Florentine bankers and borrowed the equivalent of half a million of our money. Chaucer, we know, in 1378 was in Genoa, Milan, and Florence on political business. He found all Florence ringing with the praise of Dante, the great exile, who was now the Great Master, and whom he afterwards commemorated with such reverence. It therefore seems more than likely that Chaucer heard, and knew, the Florentine songs at first hand, for considering the success they enjoyed, surely his Florentine hosts would have been at pains to show a distinguished foreigner that in music, as in other arts, they were in front of, and not behind, the rest of Europe. The chances, therefore, seem in favour of the *Ars Nova* songs having trickled through to England; but whatever may have been the case with Dunstable, his pupils Binchois and Dufay certainly knew them, either at the Court of Philip of Burgundy, or, Dufay especially, when he became a singer in the Papal choir in Rome. The *Ars Nova* was about to become the great school of counterpoint in foreign hands, though often on Italian soil. It also had accomplished something else, for it had opened the way for what we may perhaps call the humanist side of music, that side which was to appeal so strongly to posterity. The old impersonal attitude of devotion still dominated certain composers, but new paths were being opened, and a new spirit moved through the world: the spirit which demanded that music should be a means for the expression of personal emotion, and for the feelings of a human world. Henceforth there are two currents in Italian music, one of the Church, one of the Court, which run side by side, often intermingling, sometimes at variance, but persisting all through the Renaissance, until we find them again in many of the great musical works of modern times.

II

THE RISE OF CHORAL MUSIC

Musica continuo versatur in ore deorum
Musica circumfert concorde cardine coelos
Musica plante Deo nostros compaginat artus.

FOLENGO

THE greatest event of the later fourteenth century was the return to Rome of Pope Gregory XI in 1377. He found the Eternal City devastated by civil feuds; the brief triumph of Rienzi had ended in tragedy a few years earlier; many of the most beautiful buildings were fast going to ruin, and, compared to other Italian towns, Rome had but little to offer in the way of art or culture. The Papal Court at Avignon had been a centre of learning, the Pope's choir had attracted many musicians, and these now followed the Court to Rome. By this time the *Ars Nova* was famous, and composers had quickly understood the immense possibilities that were open to them. A whole generation of musicians sprang up in England and in Flanders, and, for the composers of the latter country especially, one of the chief schools was the Papal choir. Here they received every facility and encouragement: choral music was fast becoming the fashion, and in an amazingly short time its technique was brought to perfection.

The first figure which meets us at this period is that of Dufay, one of the many 'Fathers of Music'. He was born about 1400 and, with Binchois, seems to have been a pupil of Dunstable. He certainly must have known the works of Marchetto di Padova, and when he came to Rome in 1428 he had every opportunity of hearing all the music of Italy. He was a Papal singer until 1437, when he went to the Court of Philip the Good, Duke of Burgundy, and from thence to Cambrai as canon of the Cathedral, where he died. Dufay's great pupil, Okeghem, was also a great teacher, and Hobrecht, Brumel, Pierre La Rue, and Josquin de Près all studied under him. Brumel and Hobrecht were both at the Court of Ferrara, for the Pope's choir may have been the most important one in Italy, but every prince took a pride in his own 'cappella' and sought to obtain the best possible singers and musicians. San Lorenzo in Florence was famous for its music, and at the Courts of Mantua, Ferrara, and Milan every art was encouraged, while Venice could boast of a European musical reputation. The Pope was also constantly on the move, for political reasons, to different places, and the best members of his choir certainly accompanied their master; thus new musical ideas could be interchanged and standards of performance compared.

In 1409 Pope Martin V was in Siena and Florence, where he received the homage of the anti-pope; and there is a fresco on the façade of Sant' Egidio representing his consecration of that church. Florence was then at the height of her power under Cosimo I, and her wealth and art were displayed to the admiration of all the world. Thither in 1439 came the Emperor John Paleologus and the Patriarch Joseph of Constantinople to meet the Pope, Eugenius IV, for the Council which was to unite Christendom, and we see their gorgeous procession in the Benozzo Gozzoli frescoes of the Riccardi Chapel. How beautiful the city must have appeared to them, with its wonderful buildings, its churches and convents, palaces and bridges! Cosimo may well have been proud to show his guests all that was being done. San Lorenzo and Santa Maria Novella were already famous, and he had but lately undertaken to rebuild San Marco, causing the work to be done by Michelozzo, whilst Fra Angelico had been brought from Fiesole to decorate its walls. Brunelleschi was at the height of his career, and the great Church of Santa Maria del Fiore had been successfully finished. Already the brothers of the splendid Society of the Misericordia could be seen going about the streets on their errands of mercy. Ghiberti was working on the doors of the baptistery, while Donatello, Luca della Robbia, Jacopo della Quercia, Gentile da Fabriano, Masaccio, Andrea del Castagno, and many others were almost daily producing beautiful works, showing the truth of Vasari's words that 'To Florence more than any other place came men perfect in every art'.

We surely cannot doubt that for such an important occasion every effort would be made to produce the finest music available, both for the long Church services and the civil ceremonies. All must have wished to impress the foreign visitors, both by the beauty of the music itself and by the excellence of the singing. The new contrapuntal art could hardly fail to produce its effect, as the voices rose and fell in a way hitherto unknown, which must have been enchanting to ears unaccustomed to it.

The first composer really to perfect the art of choral writing was Josquin de Près, the direct forerunner of Orlando di Lasso and Palestrina. In 1486 he was a singer in the Papal choir, and afterwards in Ferrara before returning to Cambrai. Josquin's fame was enormous. 'Prince of music', his contemporaries declared, saying 'that no one knows as he does how to excite the emotions of the soul by his songs'. This is great praise, and once and for all should dispel our notion that the music of a past age was 'dry', or written only for scholastic effect. Music has always been written to satisfy the emotional needs of its hearers, and all great music has attained this end, even if by different means from those we are accustomed to.

It is our lack of perception which hampers us so grievously when listening to music of another age. We expect the shade of emotion which later centuries have given us, we want, unconsciously perhaps, the sentiment to which we are accustomed. In general we use our imagination less in regard to music than any other art. We do not fail to recognize and love the beauty of Duccio and the Sienese painters, for instance, because their technique was different from that of Raphael and later masters, yet all too often we are utterly deaf and unresponsive to the charm, the enchanting humour, and the deep tenderness there is in these older composers. It is true we are unused to their musical language, but, after all, a little patience and insight will help us to overcome that difficulty. The Madrigal singers, the Société des Instruments Anciens, Mr. Dolmetsch and his followers, and Madame Wanda Landowska have shown us what treasures we habitually ignore, and many of the recent publications of old music have helped us with the practical difficulty of reading it correctly, arriving at the right *tempo*, and understanding its finer nuances. We complacently talk of music as a 'modern' art, and the extraordinary document launched by Dr. Richard Strauss in 1921 (Manifesto of Fontainebleau) declares that all the art of the past has served but to lead to our present perfection, by which he would seem to imply that the history of music can be represented as a plain rising to a pinnacle. It is far more like a chain of uneven mountains. Nor is Dr. Strauss alone, for Dr. Burney in the eighteenth century had very much the same idea. Fétis, writing in 1883, was nearer the truth in insisting rather on development than on progress in music. Every different style of music must have a rise and fall, a period often of transformation into something else, but each style at its highest has produced perfect works. Individual taste can prefer and exalt one or other, and has not time shown us repeatedly what a fugitive thing is taste, and especially taste in music?

The Rise of Choral Music

The Greeks had a perfect and finished musical art, to judge by what they wrote of it, and even Homer gives us a picture of three different singers. There is Phemius the renowned 'lifting up his voice in sweet sound'. Demodocus, the blind singer who made Odysseus weep, and the unfortunate minstrel into whose care Agamemnon gave Clytemnestra. How beautiful, too, are some of the old Hebrew songs, yet Voltaire was capable of declaring that, in the time of Louis XIV, music, the already hoary-headed Muse, was 'in its cradle', and a like ignorance is shown by countless writers and musicians! There is this excuse for ignorance about music, that it is much harder to teach and to know than any other art. Many of the compositions of the great Flemish and Italian masters were published in Rome early in the sixteenth century, and since have been reproduced in modern editions. Many more lie hidden and unknown in the great libraries of Europe, though happily there is now a more general interest and desire to bring them to light, and perform them in such a way that we may realize the great beauty of much that has hitherto been forgotten. Music must be heard to be appreciated, and no writing about it is of any use unless it can be thus brought to new life.

Much has been done in these last years, and in Westminster Cathedral, in Saint Sulpice, Saint Eustache, and the *Scola Cantorum* in Paris and other places Josquin de Près and his contemporaries have proved what an unfailing appeal their works can make to our sense of choral beauty. In this art they were indeed masters, and the achievements of the *Ars Nova* were soon left behind. Choral music developed in a perfectly symmetrical way, and to give any idea of the effects it aimed at I cannot do better than quote Sir Hubert Parry's words. Speaking of the composers, he says: 'Their artistic instinct was especially attracted by the fascinating effect of diverse movement, controlled into the unity of a perfect flow of harmony. To them it was still essential that each individual voice part should be pleasurable to sing, and the more subtly the independence of each singer or voice part was suggested, the more fascinating was the artistic effect. The result was that in one phase of this kind of art composers aimed chiefly at making the accents and climaxes of the various voice parts constantly alternate with one another. One part rose when another fell, one held a note when another moved, one came to its highest climax at one moment and then descended, while another, as it were overlapping, moved up in its turn to another climax and then in its turn gave way. And as the skill of composers in managing these progressions improved, they found out how to distribute the climaxes of the various voice parts so as to make them gain in vital warmth by coming ever closer and closer; and the hearer could, in a moderate degree, be excited by the sound of successive crises in different qualities of tone, sometimes tenor, sometimes treble, sometimes bass; each of which seemed successively to rise into prominence within the smooth texture of the harmonious flow of sound, and then to be merged into it as another voice took its place.' It was a great gain to contrapuntal music that it still lay under the sway of the modes, and was ruled by harmonic and melodic considerations and not by tonality. As yet the few accidentals used were introduced because certain intervals were recognized as unpleasing, not to obtain a change of key, for the idea of modulation, as Sir Hubert further points out, 'was alien to the very heart of the modal system'.

The subtle beauty of modal harmony and melody are triumphantly shown in this great school of pure choral music, and its sense of rest and power is largely due to its calm and even rhythm. Whilst composers were writing, as all these were, Masses, Psalms, Motets, Magnificats and Antiphons in many parts, there was no need of a strong rhythmical accent corresponding to our heavy beat of the bar, and here, too, the rhythm of Plainsong was exerting its hidden influence. Every part rose and fell with a surge and an ebb, but not with a recurring accent, which would only have disturbed the balance of the whole. Secular compositions, of which there were many, especially madrigals, were written in the same style as sacred music, somewhat enlivened, and often with expression; but in the earlier stage of contrapuntal art the difference was not great, and it took some time before secular choral music yielded to the definite influence of dance music.

Josquin de Près exerted a great influence on Italian

musical life, not only by his own works but through his pupil Adrian Willaert, commonly known as Messer Adriano. In 1516 he went to Rome, presumably to seek the coveted post of Papal singer; but he must have been disappointed, for we hear of him in Ferrara and, after some years, in Venice, as organist of Saint Mark's. This position was one which every musician envied. Saint Mark's had always been famous for its music and for the excellent double organ which now inspired Messer Adriano to write for a double choir. It was the first time any such attempt had been made, but many of the Venetian masters followed his example with great success. He was succeeded as organist and choirmaster by his pupils Cipriano da Rore, Vicentino, and the Gabrielis, with whom the Venetian school, both of choral and instrumental composition, rose to its height at the end of the sixteenth century. The whole musical atmosphere and outlook of Venice was quite different from that of Rome—different as were the two cities.

We must leave Venice, however, for the moment, and turn back to Rome, where choral music was soon to attain its purest beauty in the wonderful works of Palestrina. His contemporary, the other great composer of the contrapuntal school, Orlando di Lasso, 'the Belgian Orpheus', lies almost entirely outside Italy, and although he was in Sicily and Milan with Ferdinando Gonzaga, his life was spent chiefly in Flanders and Germany. He undoubtedly absorbed a great deal of Italian influence, the love of beautiful sounds for their own sakes, and the singableness of the voice parts, adding this to the technical ability of the Flemish school. It was, indeed, a union of these two, Italian sense of beauty and Flemish art, which combined to make the works of Festa and Palestrina so remarkable.

Costanzo Festa has been overshadowed by his great follower, but he was the first prominent Italian composer of his school, for hitherto the foremost masters had been chiefly from beyond the Alps. He was attached to the choir of St. Peter's in 1517 and died in 1545. He produced a considerable amount of music, including the famous *Te Deum* which is still sung in St. Peter's. Festa's style of composition is nearly akin to that of Palestrina, and it was he and Giovanni Animuccia who undoubtedly most influenced the young Pierluigi.

I had not meant to touch upon this, the greatest Italian master and one of the greatest composers of the world, for his life is by now well known and has been most ably discussed. It is impossible, however, not to do so, for Italian music of the Renaissance centres round him, and he is as much the outcome of Italian life and Art as Michelangelo or Leonardo. He stands now, as then, the supreme master of Italian music, who carried choral music to a height which has never been surpassed. Here we find the grandest inspiration united to the grandest beauty and design, and such complete technical mastery that all sense of technique disappears. Those endless complicated voice parts rise and fall, and cross each other, in the most intricate patterns, and yet the whole design emerges large and natural and inevitable, the perfect expression of a sublime idea. Palestrina has the true Italian feeling for melody and beauty, and also the true Italian value of the individual parts, whilst his line and architectural structure is as great and apparently simple as the art of Brunelleschi. Pierluigi, or, as he is more generally known from the name of his native town, Palestrina, was born about 1524 and went early to Rome, where he had the opportunity of hearing, and perhaps studying, with the best singers and composers. He may even have known Arcadelt, a famous Flemish musician who was choirmaster of the Cappella Giulia about that time.

Rome, under Clement VII, was recovering from the devastation caused by the siege of Charles V in 1527. For a hundred years war and peace had alternated in and around the Eternal City, and after the return of the Papacy from Avignon it had been harassed by the schism of the West, only finally healed in 1449. Nicolas V, besides founding the present Vatican Library, had begun the urgent work of restoration to the almost crumbling churches, and planned the complete reconstruction of Saint Peter's. The design for this colossal enterprise was entrusted to Rosellino and Gian Battista Alberti, an artist who thought of architecture in terms of harmony, and declared that every building must be 'una bella musica'. After the death of Nicolas V, one art-loving Pope succeeded another, and Pius IV, Sixtus IV, to whom the Sistine Chapel is due, and Alexander VI all helped on the advancement of the church and adjoining Vatican Palace.

Julius II, however, dissatisfied with the plans of his predecessors, and encouraged by Bramante and San Gallo, ordered them to make a completely new design for Saint Peter's on a far grander scale, by which it was to become, indeed, the greatest and richest church that Renaissance art could conceive. He laid the foundation-stone of this new building in 1506 and duly advised all the sovereigns of Europe of the fact. Every artist of note had been, and was, pressed into the Pope's service: Fra Angelico, Botticelli, Pinturicchio, Sodoma, Perugino, and Signorelli had all worked in Saint Peter's, and Julius II now summoned Michelangelo to Rome and commissioned Raphael to paint the Stanze and Loggie. In all this ferment of artistic activity, and the excitement of founding the Vatican Museum, and collecting priceless works of art, the obscure pilgrim, Martin Luther, who was in Rome in 1510, may well have passed unnoticed! Julius II was succeeded by Leo X in 1513, and never had the art of Rome shone so brightly, or the centre of Christendom been so outwardly gorgeous. On the death of Bramante, Raphael took up the work in Saint Peter's, but his own early death in 1520 left it in the hands of Peruzzi and of Michelangelo, whom the Pope appointed chief architect of the Basilica.

Throughout all these years music had been enthusiastically

encouraged by the Popes, and especially Leo X, who had all the Medici talent for it, and spared neither money nor pains to attract all the best composers and singers. His death in 1521 marked the end of an epoch, for at once the reforming spirit of Adrian VI made itself felt. The Vatican Gallery was walled up, the Pope looked with horror upon the 'heathen statues' collected there, and when Adrian was quickly succeeded by Clement VII, the fire of the Reformation was ablaze in the North, and the Pope had to face war and siege and poverty. During this time Palestrina seems to have been living quietly in his native town, and even as quite a young man his talent must have been recognized, for he was organist and choirmaster at the age of twenty. The work in Saint Peter's had been taken up again under Paul III, who confirmed Michelangelo in his position as chief architect, sculptor and painter, and a few years later, in 1551, Julius III called on Palestrina to take charge, first of the boys' choir of the Cappella Giulia and then to act as choirmaster, composer, and organist to the Papal choir.

Surely two such great spirits have seldom met working through different arts to a common end as the old sculptor and the young musician who almost day by day in Saint Peter's must have seen and heard each other's works. Michelangelo had lived through the Renaissance to the new spirit of the Catholic revival, and he was the friend of the first members of San Filippo Neri's 'Oratorio'. Palestrina was almost untouched by the Renaissance, and he belonged essentially to the counter-Reformation, of which his music is a great expression. He was a friend of San Filippo Neri, and through him was in touch and in sympathy with the doctrines and spiritual direction of Savonarola and Santa Caterina dei Ricci. Savonarola had had very little use for all the art and learning of the Medici Court, and the Catholic revival cared nothing for the Renaissance, and was concentrated upon spiritual values and the reforms being carried out by the Council of Trent. Palestrina doubtless knew how Savonarola had attacked the music in the churches, finding that it had become imbued with too worldly a spirit. 'Take away all your fine songs,' he had exclaimed, 'the choirs of these gentlemen are nought but a tumult; for there is one singer with a great voice like a bull, and the others yelp around him like dogs, and never a word can one hear of what they utter. Stop, therefore, all this figured music and let us sing the Plainsong music of the Church.' The question of Church music was, indeed, before the Council, and some of its members were in favour of suppressing any but Gregorian chant. The answer came with Palestrina's Mass of Papa Marcello, before which he had written the words: 'O Lord, open Thou mine eyes', and which was instantly accepted.

This music was felt to be, what it still is, a pure expression of Catholic, mystical Christianity, which worthily fulfilled its spiritual purpose, namely, to 'lift and form the minds of the faithful to all sanctity'.

Palestrina was rewarded with the honorary title of

'Maestro Compositore' of the Papal choir, which after him but one other musician, Felice Anerio, was to enjoy. When Paul IV undertook his drastic reform of the Papal Court, on his accession in 1555, he determined to sweep away the laymen from his service, and Palestrina and two other married choirmasters had the disappointment of having to leave the Cappella Giulia, and the loss of this position reduced him to such poverty that he was forced to beg for help from Sixtus V. He was offered the post of choirmaster at St. John Lateran and Santa Maria Maggiore, both of which he held, and in vain the Duke of Mantua tried to persuade him to leave Rome. This Duke of Mantua, Prince Boncompagni, and the Cardinal d' Este were all friends of Palestrina and interested in the school of composition which he had started with Animuccia and his pupils, G. M. and G. B. Nannini, at Santa Maria Maggiore. This school was most successful, and from it came Vicentino, Allegri, Cifra and many of the masters of the seventeenth century.

San Filippo Neri, who was himself such a lover of and believer in music as an essential part of the spiritual life, asked Palestrina to undertake also the musical direction of the newly-established Oratory. There, with Animuccia and Nannini, he laid the foundations of our modern Oratorio, which at first was nothing more than hymns and *laudi* on some sacred episode or text sung by the members of the Oratory. On the death of Animuccia, the post of Papal choirmaster again fell vacant, and on hearing the stupendous

Mass *Assumpta est Maria,* the Pope recalled Palestrina to his service in 1571, shortly after the death of his great colleague, Michelangelo. Sixtus V, another friend of San Filippo's, would gladly have given Palestrina charge also of the choir of the Sistine Chapel, but again a difficulty arose, for the singers would not tolerate a lay conductor. Palestrina's time, however, was fully occupied, for Gregory XIII entrusted him with the work of complete revision of all the Plainsong Offices. He was able to prepare a new edition of the *Directorium chori* and the *Graduale Romanum* and Offices for Holy Week, and the task was completed by Anerio and Suriano. Thus Palestrina's last years were all spent in the service of Saint Peter's in the Cappella Giulia, until he died in 1594, assisted by his friend and confessor, San Filippo Neri. The number of Palestrina's works is enormous, more than ninety Masses, quantities of psalms, motets, antiphons and madrigals, which have been published in thirty-four volumes by Breitkopf & Hartel, and are the best monument to such a master. Palestrina's influence was very great. Not only upon his own immediate followers and pupils, but upon musicians who in their art seem farthest, perhaps, from him. Gounod, for instance, began by thinking Palestrina's music arid, and yet came to acknowledge that he could not live without it, whilst for Wagner it was 'eine geistige offenbarung, ein zeit los, raumloses Bild'.

Surely we might apply to it especially the words of Sir Thomas Browne, that 'there is a musick wherever there is a harmony, order or proportion, and something in it of Divinity more than the ear discovers'.

Choral music of the Roman school was henceforth identified with the name of Palestrina, although, strictly speaking, he did not create the style called after him. Rome remained its stronghold, for the rest of Italy was soon far too busy running after new gods even to heed it, but Palestrina had left a new vision of music to his pupils and friends, and no other influence drew them from it.

Of his worthy followers mention must be made of Anerio, some of whose works were thought at one time to be by Palestrina; his friend Vittoria, the Spaniard, G. M. Nannini and G. B. Nannini, and his pupil Allegri, the author of the famous nine-voice *Miserere*, only sung in Saint Peter's, and which was never allowed to be copied, until a young musician named Mozart wrote it down note by note as he listened! Then come Suriano, Cifra, Valentini, Bernabei, and Bai, choir singers and masters all of them, chiefly of Saint Peter's and the other great Roman churches, and composers who faithfully carried on their tradition and, for another half-century at least, made choral music the glory of Italy, as the English composers also made it of England.

Pater has said that the art of music realizes most completely the ideal of all art in the perfect identification of matter and form. 'In its consummate moments the end is not distinct from the matter, the subject from the expression: they inhere in and completely saturate each other, and to it, therefore, to the condition of its perfect moments all the arts may be supposed constantly to tend and aspire.' Pure choral music is one of these consummate moments of the art, the top of a mountain beyond which there is no progress, although we can, and do, welcome the other heights, and different views that succeeding generations have given us.

III

INSTRUMENTS AND INSTRUMENTAL MUSIC

Now divine airs! Now is his soul ravished! Is it not strange that sheeps' guts should hale souls out of men's bodies?

STRANGE it may be, but which of us can resist the violin or 'cello in the hands of a master? And what is true of us was equally so of our ancestors of the sixteenth century. When we turn back to early Renaissance musical art, we do come, in one sense, to a rather barren field, for there is no instrumental music of that period that we know which can compare with the achievements of choral composition. Again, do not let us flatter ourselves that instrumental music is a modern production, for without going farther afield, may I only quote one passage from Seneca, already quoted by Madame Landowska in her excellent book, *Musique Ancienne:* 'See this multitude of voices which forms our great musical choirs—they are so perfectly united that the ear is only conscious of one sound. Amongst these voices some are pitched high, some medium, some low, on every degree. One hears the voices of men and women intermingled with the sounds of the flutes that accompany them. Each of these voices is, so to speak, hidden in the multitude and yet each stands out with its own particular character. Besides this great number of voices our amphitheatres are surrounded by trumpets, and our orchestras are full of an infinity of string and wind instruments of all kinds. Here is a multitude which seems to threaten a terrible discord, but do not fear, the result is a concert.'

The Romans, therefore, obviously knew all about musical performances on a big scale and the organization of an orchestra, while the flute and chitara were favourite instruments of the Greeks. The Roman orchestra disappeared with the Empire, and during the Middle Ages, when Gregorian Church music predominated, any instrumental composition was naturally eclipsed. Except in popular music, or in songs such as were sung by the Troubadours or Florentine poets, there was no need for it. Secular instrumental music, except that of the organ, has a social origin and began in the dance, whether sacred or profane. Throughout the fourteenth and fifteenth centuries it consisted almost entirely of accompaniments to the songs, and their near relations, the dances.

The very name of *ballata* shows its origin, and the *sonetto*, *canzone*, *rispetto*, *strambotto* and madrigal were all popular forms of sung lyrics, which began with simple airs and verses of the people, were taken by the poets of the *dolce stil nuovo* and made into the poetry of Art, and thus became the pastime of Society. These songs were accompanied chiefly by the vielle and lute, and each had a prelude, interlude, and postlude, which were probably more improvizations than definite compositions, for it was only when instrumental music was recognized as a channel for the expression of individual emotion and inspiration that the necessity arose for even writing it down quite accurately. This is essentially a later idea, and instrumental music, in our sense of the word, is a more modern art; but even our mightiest symphony had its beginnings far back in the accompaniments of the *ballata*, *frottola* or *sonetto*. We see the preludes, the interludes, the postludes gradually expanding and, as it were, becoming more conscious of their own importance. Sometimes they were even played without the vocal part, at last the words were dropped altogether and the dance and song between them finally yielded us the suite, the sonata, and the symphony.

If our knowledge of the actual instrumental music of the Quattrocento is very limited, not so is our knowledge of the instruments themselves. The most casual visitor to Italian museums and galleries can hardly fail to be struck by the number and variety of instruments which continually appear in the pictures, and the whole idea of music, which is so strong in the plastic arts of the Renaissance, that it is surely a good apology for that music that it was able to inspire such great works.

It may be argued that it is a purely subjective matter to apprehend one art in the terms of another, but I think many of us standing before the masterpieces of Italian painting and sculpture must often feel that they almost pass into an actual strain of music.

We come back to the passage of Pater which I have already quoted and its sequel, where he says: 'In music rather than in poetry is to be found the true type and measure of perfected art', and that such art 'is struggling after the law and principle of music to a condition that music alone completely realizes.' This is especially true where an idea or emotion dominates a picture or statue, or where the artist has achieved such inner and outer harmony in his composition, that we answer to it by an almost audible sense of melody and harmony. The musically suggestive power of the plastic arts upon the beholder, or listener I had almost said, is so great, and yet often seems to pass unnoticed.

There is a beautiful bas-relief of Luca della Robbia on the Campanile in Florence, representing Music, under the form of Orpheus charming the beasts and birds, and Harmony, of which Ruskin wrote: 'Harmony of Song; in the full power of it, meaning perfect education in all art of the Muses and of civilised life; the mystery of its concord is taken as a symbol of that of a perfect state, one day doubtless of a perfect world.' Luca achieved this concord in another great musical work, the *Cantoria*, which he made for Santa Maria del Fiore. This is no frozen music, for it is alive with the splendid vitality of concerted effort towards one end, and that end is the noblest which the human mind has ever imagined. *Laudate Dominum* is at once the motto and *raison d'être* of the masterpiece, and the voices of the singing boys unite with trumpets, lutes, harps, cymbals, strings, and pipes in a magnificent concentrated outburst of praise. All the words of the psalm, indeed, become a wonderful reality, as the whole work rises in an ordered yet triumphant music, which can hardly ever have been matched in any art.

What Luca expressed in sculpture, Fra Angelico did in painting, and it is impossible to look at his pictures without realizing what an overwhelming sense of harmony must have filled this man's whole being. Music, indeed, seems to be the keynote of his soul, and surely he, with Richard Rolle, knew 'the song when in a plenteous soul the sweetness of eternal love, with burning is taken, and thought into song is turned and the mind into full sweet sound is changed'. In all his works there is this sense and presence of music, and of perfect harmony, while very often sound almost mingles with the visible beauty of the picture. In the great Coronation of the Virgin, for instance, one nearly hears the blast of the long trumpets as their forms cross each other in the sky, and the saints seem to pause and listen to the symphony which is being played by the surrounding angel-musicians.

These are but a few illustrations of the idea of music, which has always struck me so forcibly in connection with the other arts, and each of us could multiply such examples almost indefinitely in the churches and galleries of Italy.

Instruments and Instrumental Music

Music has a place in hundreds of Renaissance paintings, from the early frescoes of the Spanish chapel in Santa Maria Novella to the engrossing 'Concert' of the Pitti, formerly ascribed to Giorgione.

Instruments of all kinds are constantly in the hands of the angels who surround the Madonna and Child, and how often we meet Saint Cecilia, with her organ or lute! Banquets, marriage processions, and those wonderful and fascinating *trionfi:* all have their attendant musicians, and sometimes a lute hangs even in the cell of Saint Jerome or the retreat of a hermit.

These paintings do more than merely show that their creators had a deep love of music, and for us they have an immense practical value, for they show more clearly than anything the different instruments which were in use at the time. From them we see the amount and variety of the instruments which must have been played during the fifteenth century, for the Italians have always had, not only fine taste in instrumental music, but a great talent for the construction of the instruments themselves, and long before the days of great Amati, Guarnieri, and Stradivarius, ingenious craftsmen were at work constantly experimenting. In the pictures of the early Florentine, Sienese, and Venetian masters there are harps, viols, pipes, trombones, lutes, trumpets, cembali, drums, and organs, a whole orchestra in fact, and from them it is often easy to trace the whole development of the individual instrument.

Let us take the viola, for instance, and its elder relations the vielle and rebec, so much used as an accompaniment to the early songs. They were the ancestors of the violin, and their technique was that of a rudimentary fiddle. In the earlier pictures the viole were large-bodied and short-necked, but in Italy, the home of viola playing, they soon became longer and more like the violin as we know it. Two distinct classes of viola developed later: the Viola da Braccia and the Viola da Gamba, and from them sprang all the stringed instruments of the modern orchestra, with the exception of the harp. Italian viola players were soon famous throughout Europe, and they travelled far and wide. We hear of them in England being received by Henry VIII, and François I had three of them, Paolo da Milano, Niccolo and Domenico di Lucca, in constant attendance upon him.

Before the full development of the violin the lute, however, was the most popular of all stringed instruments. It originated probably in Spain and was brought to Italy and to Florence by *virtuosi* attached to the Court of Aragon. Here Charles VIII and his successors heard it and carried it back with them to France, to charm the Courts of Fontainebleau and Saint Germain. It was the aristocrat of all that family of instruments which includes the guitar, the banjo, and the mandoline, and it possessed a very rich original literature. It was the instrument of Society, of pleasant songs or intricate dance tunes. Lovers sang their serenades to its accompaniment, princes and poets alike learned to play it.

The lute had six strings tuned in fourths, with a third in the centre, Sol, Do, Fa, La, Re, Sol; but there was also a smaller variety of only four strings. Together with the organ it was the first instrument to have a tablature of its own, and its music is especially remarkable as having been always founded upon a chromatic basis. Later on, it took the most fantastic forms, as is shown by Piero di Cosimo in a picture of Perseus freeing Andromeda, in the Uffizi Gallery. There is a group of musicians at one side, one of whom holds a long instrument, curved and graceful in shape, while another has pipes not unlike those of a bag-pipes fastened to the body of his lute. It must have been extraordinarily complicated to play, and reminds one somewhat of those marvellous instruments still sometimes to be heard at street corners, or in little back 'piazzette', and which seem to combine every known instrument in one astounding medley!

To the lute family belonged that strange instrument, the Pentekontachordon, invented by Fabio Colonna about 1567. It had seventeen strings, and each note had three and the octave seventeen tonal divisions. The lute was the only instrument to have an independent music written for it as early as the fifteenth century. Tinctoris mentions Petrus Bonus as a celebrated lute-player at the Court of Ferrara, and a quantity of lute music was composed in all countries during the next century. In Italy there were Ambrogio Dalza, whose *Intabolatura di lauto* dates from 1508, Francesco di Milano, Antonio Rotta, Melchiorre di Barberio, Domenico Bianchini, and many others, and the lute was *par excellence* the instrument of secular music. It took the place of the piano of to-day. It was to be found in almost every home, its transcriptions of popular songs were the equivalent of our modern piano operatic scores, its dances and airs were the delight of prince and burgher, the pastime of anyone with musical talent.

For distinguished ancestry the harp could certainly surpass the other string instruments, and two varieties were in use during the fifteenth century. The large one of twenty strings played with the hand is one of the oldest of all instruments, and akin to the lyre of poetry, and, we may presume, to the harps of the Elders in the Apocalypse. In the smaller kind, known as the tympanum or dulcimer, the strings were stretched across a sounding-board and hit with hammers, not unlike tiny drumsticks. To anyone who has had the pleasure of hearing the tympanum well played, it must seem extraordinary that it should ever have passed from general favour. The range is small, but in its own limited space it speaks with a voice whose silvery perfection could compare with any invention of later date. Of the same class as the tympanum, and not unlike to it in the principles of their construction, were the clavichord and, later, the cembalo. Afterwards, in the hands of the great instrument builders we see the dulcimer left far behind, while the clavichord and cembalo grew ever more important, until they became indispensable as the accompaniment of the violin or voice in the delicate chamber music of the seventeenth and eighteenth centuries.

Wind instruments are almost as general as the viole and lute in countless pictures of the Renaissance, and, indeed, ever since the days of Joshua the blast of the trumpet seems to have been the instrumental equivalent of the great shout of the people. It is impossible to mistake the character of the trumpet, and for that reason, perhaps, it has always played a very definite part in man's imagination and in actual life. Saint John likened the voice of an angel to the sound of the trumpet ringing through Heaven, and on earth it is the natural herald of proclamations, a means of calling men to battle or of stirring them to any unwonted interest. During the Renaissance it was used upon many occasions, both great and small. Conquerors marched to its sound, so did peaceful wedding processions, as we see on many a marriage *cassone*, and even the different dishes in a banquet were often ushered into the room by a fanfare. The trumpet, too, is almost the only instrument whose form and technique seem never to have substantially changed, and which may be said to have been born fully grown. There are trumpets on the Ghiberti doors of the Baptistery in Florence, and, in Giotto and Fra Angelico paintings, trombones in a picture of a Florentine marriage which are very like ours, and we can almost hear them sounding as we imagine the gay procession crossing the Piazza.

How much, indeed, we owe to these painters of the Renaissance, who have shown us all these instruments in their daily life and use, so that they need never be for us dusty old things standing in the corner of a museum!

I have left the greatest of wind instruments, the organ, to the last, for, owing to its privileged position as the instrument of the Church, it played a great part in the history of music. The organ was well known before the coming of Christ; Julian the Apostate possessed one, Saint Augustine speaks of it, the Emperor Constantine gave one to King Pepin. Organ-building was cultivated in some of the great monasteries, where it was used to accompany the Plainsong. Its mechanical development was rapid, and early in the fourteenth century pedals were added to the small, original compass, and the portable organs that we see in so many pictures gave way to the big fixture which became the king of instruments. In Italy, as we have seen, Venice was famous both for its organs and organists, and there exists the register of every organist in Saint Mark's from the early Trecento onwards.

The whole artistic life of the Republic might, indeed, have dazzled the rest of Europe, as year by year Venice seemed to grow more beautiful, and her wonderful buildings and pictures to increase. Many of the great Venetian painters were lovers of music. Giorgione was himself an excellent musician, and Sansovino could truly say that 'Music really has her home in this city'. The Venetians were equally interested in choral and instrumental music: they made collections of instruments, and organized concerts, and a critical public helped to maintain a very high standard of musical life. Every incentive was given to Art: the Doge's choir and music of Saint Mark's had to be worthy of that great church; there were constant instrumental concerts, and any new ideas which could enhance the brilliance of Venetian life were eagerly encouraged.

Venetian musicians had also the good fortune to live in a city where printing was an art and the printing-press renowned. Ottaviano Petrucci was born at Fossombrone, near Urbino, in 1466, but it was in Venice that he first made use of his new invention of printing musical notes, and he worked there just about the time that the Neacademia of Ser Aldo was exciting Sabellico and all the Venetian literary world. Petrucci afterwards moved to Rome and became the well-known music publisher there of the school of Palestrina, but the Venetian business was carried on by Amadeo Scotto and Niccolò da Rafael. Petrucci's work was an immense advantage to Italian musicians, and a large amount of French and Flemish music was also printed in Venice. Petrucci's collections of songs and madrigals are famous, and it is thanks to him that much of the music of that time has been preserved. Later on, the Gardano family had a renowned musical printing-press and published a quantity of music, and all this activity certainly helped to make Venice one of the most living musical centres of Europe.

Messer Adriano had attracted many northerners to Venice by his music, and he was followed by a number of distinguished pupils: Cipriano da Rore, famous for his strong chromatic tendency and the romantic quality of his music; Guami, Annibale Padovano, Vicentino, Claudio Merulo, Donati, Costanzo Porta, Deruta Zarlino, and Andrea and Giovanni Gabrieli, and many others who became organists and choirmasters in the cities of Northern Italy.

Zarlino was born in 1517 with marked intellectual gifts; he became very well known in many ways, for he was learned in philosophy, poetry, and mathematics. He joined the Franciscan Order, but was Choirmaster of Saint Mark's, though, unfortunately, many of his sacred compositions have been lost. His fame is as the greatest theoretical musician of the sixteenth century, and his book, *Istituzioni Harmoniche e Dimostrazioni Harmoniche*, is an excellent treatise on counterpoint, and lays the foundations of modern harmony. He bases harmonic law, not on the modes, but on the major and minor scales, and all subsequent writers on the subject derive their ideas from him. He wished to carry his harmonic principles into practice, and at his suggestion Domenico di Pesaro made a kind of clavichord, with different keys for the quarter-tones, that is, for A sharp and B flat. The compromise of the 'well-tempered clavichord' was yet far to seek. Zarlino was an intimate friend of Tintoretto, and he was very much considered and honoured during his lifetime as the most prominent Venetian musician. There were tremendous rejoicings in Venice in 1571 for the Victory of Lepanto, when the Turks were defeated under the Doge Luigi Mocenigo, and Zarlino was called upon to celebrate the great occasion. Already musicians were turning to the drama in these festivities, and Zarlino composed the music to the poem of *Orpheus* to commemorate the victory of the Republic. When Henri III visited Venice three years later, huge entertainments were given in his honour, and *Orpheus* was performed with many other poems set to music by Zarlino. Their success was such that when Mazarin wished to introduce Italian music into France, Zarlino's *Orfeo* was what he chose, to show the French the value of the Italian musicians' art. Zarlino died in 1589, and all eyes then turned to his contemporaries, Claudio Merulo and Andrea and Giovanni Gabrieli. The Gabrielis came of an old Venetian family, and after studying with Messer Adriano, Andrea became choirmaster and organist in Saint Mark's, a post he shared with Merulo, and afterwards with his nephew Giovanni. Hassler and Heinrich Schütz came from Germany to study under these masters, and Schütz said afterwards of Giovanni, 'I passed my first years of musical study with the great Giovanni Gabrieli. Oh, immortal gods, what a man this Giovanni was! If the Muses had taken husbands, Melpomene would surely only have chosen him as her spouse.' The works of all these three musicians, but especially of Giovanni, were very remarkable. Totally different from the Roman school, both in idea and design, they show a great sense of brilliance and effect: many are for two and three choirs, which are used with vivid contrast and most splendid results.

The Gabrielis, in their choral music, in which they were very great masters, had not the impersonal detachment, the soaring, spiritual quality of Palestrina: they were less transcendental but more realistic and more dramatic. Many of Giovanni Gabrieli's effects were obtained by his great skill in mixing the different modes, and although he makes but little attempt at modulation in our sense of the word, yet he avoids any feeling of monotony.

What a magnificent piece of choral writing is the sixteen-voice chorus, 'Ascendit Deus in jubilo'! and when Gabrieli used chromatic effects, as in the beautiful *Miserere*, it was to heighten the expression of the words. Writing in 1555, Vicentino had said in the *Antica musica ridotta alla moderna pratica:* 'In song, music has no other object than to express by the aid of sounds the thoughts and emotions which are contained in the words.' This idea governed all Gabrieli's vocal music and that of his contemporaries, whilst fifty years later Monteverde applied it with the full force of his genius to the opera. Giovanni Gabrieli will always remain a great master of choral music, but he was also one of the first composers of solo instrumental music.

We have seen how from the song accompaniments there slowly emerged the instrumental solo, and organists such as those of the Venetian school obviously needed regular organ pieces. At first they were probably content with *versetti*, such as all Italian organists still interpose between the verses of psalms and canticles. The *versetto* was probably convenient as a means of giving a tired choir a moment's rest, but, anyhow, they were amongst the first written organ pieces, and were in the Plainsong modes. Then whole choral pieces would be transcribed for the organ, and amongst the early compositions many have the title of some psalm or hymn or motet. As the organists became more ambitious, we have the *ricercare*, the *canzone* and the *toccata*, the first of which were Claudio Merulo's two volumes published in 1598 and which added considerably to his already wide fame.

Giovanni Gabrieli was still more original, and his sonatas for three violins are a landmark in musical history. With them instrumental music enters upon a new epoch: it rises to a new level and, independent of all restrictions, the way lies open up to the greatest productions of orchestral composition. Such has been the service that Venice and Saint Mark's rendered to the art of music.

Not only Venice, however, but other towns also in the north of Italy could boast of their music during the sixteenth century. Bologna and Verona had established musical societies; Maschera and the Antegnati family were famous organists and composers in Brescia. Rossi, who also wrote instrumental trio sonatas in Mantua, Bertaldo and Porta in Padua, Luzzaschi in Ferrara, Guami and Diruta in Venice and Lucca, and, greatest of all, Girolamo Frescobaldi. He was born in Ferrara in 1583 and died in Rome in 1644. He was a pupil of Luzzaschi and undoubtedly the greatest *virtuoso* of his time. His travels took him as far as Flanders, and he held the position of organist in several Italian Courts, besides that of Saint Peter's in Rome. There, thirty thousand people are said to have gathered to hear him, for no other artist could rival him, and the new style of organ-playing that he had cultivated. His reputation was so great that Frohberger, then Court Organist in Vienna, was given leave solely that he might come to Rome and study under Frescobaldi. His works are innumerable and show him as a fine composer of instrumental music. His fugues are masterly in their technique and structure, and well justify Bach's reverence for his great predecessor. There are brilliant *toccate*, *fantasie*, *canzoni*, *ricercari*, and *arie*, which never grow old in their wealth of variety and feeling. Many of them, together with other works of this period, are to be found in the excellent modern publication of L. Torchi's *L'Arte Musicale in Italia*. For the lover of music this collection is invaluable, and endless beautiful compositions come to life in its pages.

Once the hold of pure choral music was weakened, and the possibilities of instrumental composition had taken possession of the musicians' minds, it was not long before they thought of combining the two, to a far greater degree than had hitherto been the custom. This idea had been developing in all the North Italian composers, and a few voices united to a much larger instrumental part was what they now aimed at. Adriano Banchieri, a Bolognese pupil of Guami, and Viadana, a pupil of Porta, definitely inaugurated this new style of sacred music, for their works were the first to be written for only two or three voices with the accompaniment of a figured bass.

In a few short years they changed the course of Church music. Viadana entitled his work as 'Una invenzione commoda per ogni sorte di cantori e per gli organisti', but it was more than that. It was the opening of another view of sacred music, revealing endless new possibilities, eloquently illustrated by the beauty of Viadana's many compositions and by the great works of his successors. Banchieri was an Olivetan monk, and one of the foremost organists and composers, besides writing a number of theoretical pamphlets. He was one of the first to use a thorough definite bass, and his *Concerti Ecclesiastici*, published in 1595, are the earliest known compositions in which the figured bass appears. He was a most 'modern' and active composer of sonatas, motets, madrigals, and dramatic scenes in the madrigal style, and he also founded the Academia dei Floridi in Bologna, which afterwards, in the eighteenth century, became the celebrated Academia dei Filomusi.

Perhaps it was difficult to get enough good singers, especially in smaller places, and patiently train a choir for all the demands of contrapuntal singing, or it may have seemed a pleasant novelty to listen to a lighter voice part with an instrumental accompaniment. It was certainly easier and simpler to perform, and made less demands on the choir, if more on the organist. The sway of pure choral music was ended amongst the Lombard and Venetian musicians: the figured bass had, indeed, come to stay, and it ruled triumphantly for more than two centuries in sacred and secular music. Some people, indeed, complained loudly that the churches were 'full of the noisy sounds of trumpets, cornets and fifes', and all our sympathy is with them. They doubtless felt that much of the dignity and grandeur of choral music was being sacrificed, but the new development was inevitable, and, in its turn, led to magnificent results.

One of the chief reasons for the rapid growth of instrumental music and the number of *virtuosi* in the North of Italy was the perfection which the instruments themselves attained in the hands of the Amati, Guarnieri, and Stradivarii. These wonderful instrument makers were craftsmen in the same sense as the metal-workers, the carvers, and weavers of the Renaissance. The beauty of design, the perfection of workmanship, the patience and love of the handicraft were the same. As the artists' 'bottega' had been the school for countless works of genius, so the workshops of Cremona were the school of perfect musical instruments, and their creators are well worthy to rank with Verrocchio or Benvenuto Cellini. To enter into the details of Italian instrument making, or to follow the glorious course of later instrumental music, would take us far beyond the limits of the

Renaissance, and I can but hand the reader on to Vernon Lee's delightful *Studies of the Eighteenth Century in Italy*, where she deals so well with the musical life, and to the works of Mr. Dent and other scholars.

Much of the instrumental music of the earlier Renaissance was but the prelude to the grand achievements of the seventeenth and eighteenth centuries, when instrumental music appeared in its full beauty, ready to take its place beside all other great art. There we meet a host of famous names, Marcello, Durante, Tartini, Corelli, Vivaldi, Vitali, Porpora, Leo, Pergolesi, the Scarlatti, and how many others! No one else in musical art can give us just what these masters do. What can be grander or more moving than, for instance, the *chaconne* of Vitali, or the psalms of Marcello; more brilliant than the *concerti* of Vivaldi; more tender than many of the *arie?* Italian music at its best has always a wonderful emotional dignity, a sense of beauty of phrase and tone and construction, which makes it the worthy sister of Italian architecture and sculpture and painting.

IV

MUSIC AT THE COURTS OF ITALY

Florence and Ferrara

'In music thou shalt find rest from the great weariness of the world.'

'Whoever is harmonically composed delights in harmony.'

ONE of the most agreeable pastimes is surely the pleasure we derive from association. A name, a view, a form, a few bars of music, or often far slighter things, are able to awaken in us a whole period of history; and what romance is equal to the past we create for ourselves? I have said 'create', for it is apt to be very different from that which meets us in the pages of history: we take and we leave what we choose, but what joy our imaginary picture can give us! Probably all of us have made such imaginary pictures of the Renaissance Courts of Italy, collected from odds and ends of reading, from the sight of buildings like the Doge's Palace, or the grim Este Fortress at Ferrara, from Benozzo Gozzoli frescoes, Veronese or Titian pictures, or a page from Poliziano or Pico della Mirandola. It is all stored away somewhere in our minds, and at the words Medici, Gonzaga, Este we are back in all the brilliance and charm of Quattro- and Cinquecento Court life. There is no doubt that it was very brilliant, and we can happily ignore its dark and terrible side and turn to Music and Poetry, the twin sisters by which all that was most lovable in Renaissance life sought expression.

The Medici Court in Florence from the first had been an intellectual and artistic circle. It could not well have been otherwise, considering the amazing artistic vitality of Florence, and Cosimo the Elder, conscious, perhaps, that, after all, his family was something of the *nouveau riche*, was the patron and friend of all the great artists of the Quattrocento. He wished, in beautiful things, to leave a memorial to himself. Did he not say, 'I know the humours of this city—fifty years will not pass before we are driven out, but the buildings will remain'? The Medici's power lasted for something like three hundred years, and Cosimo lived to indulge all his artistic and literary enthusiasm, as the centre of a revival of which, in his younger days, even he could scarcely have dreamed.

Already, at the end of the Trecento, public interest in classical studies had been aroused, and the Florentine 'Studium' sent the famous invitation to Chrysoloras in Constantinople to come and fill the chair of Greek Letters. With his acceptance there began a new era, and intercourse with the East, and especially with the Greeks, increased steadily. A host of *litterati* and scholars followed their masters to Florence for the Council of Eastern and Western Christianity. The Churches remained divided, the Pope returned to Rome, the Eastern rulers to their own lands, but the welcome they had received from the Florentines remained in their memories, for where they had come as strangers they left as friends.

Not many years afterwards, in 1453, when Mahomet II besieged Constantinople, some of these same men found themselves homeless fugitives flying for their lives; and they turned to Italy, and especially to Florence, as to a second home. Nor were they disappointed; and soon the Greek scholars were listened to and sought after by an ever-widening circle of admirers, to whom the Hellenic culture was almost as intoxicating as new wine in its novelty and splendour. The manuscripts and works of art the Greeks were able to bring with them helped to fan the flame of enthusiasm, and they opened to the receptive and cultivated Latin mind the vast treasure-house of Greek learning. 'The discovery by man of himself and the universe' was, indeed, a dazzling view to those who looked out on it for the first time since the Middle Ages, and the Platonic Academy, founded by Cosimo the Elder, was the hot-house of the Humanists, disciples of Plato, who found in the religion of love and beauty a solution for the mysteries of the universe, the 'solemn harmonies of unearthly music'.

The Greek idea of music was very definite. Plato had given a perfect definition of rhythm when he said 'Rhythm is order in movement', and he and Pythagoras and other Greek philosophers claimed for music a place in all education. They made the great distinction between elevating and debasing harmony, which caused restrictions to be placed on the study of music, especially by the young. Music could be the speech of the soul, but it could be also the means for a betrayal of all finer instincts, a play of the emotions ungoverned by reason, a danger and a nuisance. This distinction was taken up by all the Italian Humanists, and it has lasted well on to our own day, for, indeed, it is a fundamental æsthetic problem that most of us do not face and certainly do not solve.

The Greeks had not only written about music, but had had an elaborate and perfected system of musical theory and practice. Aristoxenes had insisted, in regard to intervals, that experience must take the place of mathematical calculation, and that the ear must be the final judge of what was pleasing in sound. They had both choral and instrumental music, and if the Florentines did not actually hear any original Greek compositions, they must have known about them all that it was possible to know. They did not try at once to imitate Greek music, they were too spontaneous a people for that, but what they had heard must have influenced all their outlook on music, and they thought of their own musical art as probably satisfying all the demands of antiquity.

Music, with the other arts, was swept along by the rising tide of humanism, and soon became the fashion in the brilliant philosophical circle of the Medici. That circle had its spiritual aspect, as, for instance, in women such as Lucrezia Tornabuoni, Lorenzo's mother, of whom we have a charming account: writing carols and songs for her children, and taking them every day to hear Vespers sung in a neighbouring church.

She was the friend of the saintly prior of San Marco, and Archbishop, afterwards known as Sant' Antonino, the Florentine apostle of peace and charity to all men. To his insight and kindness was due the society of the 'Good men of Saint Martin', whose mission was especially to search out and relieve the 'poveri vergognosi', those who were in want and would not beg.

Sant' Antonino was followed by a very different type of man in the great prior Savonarola. Even he, in his few spare moments from the crushing task of reforming Florence, loved music, and himself wrote *laudi* in his cell in San Marco, while Fra Serafino Razzi, another Dominican, has left us a large number of exquisite spiritual songs. Several of the most ardent of the Renaissance Platonists died in the habit of Saint Dominic, and these men sought to see the services of the Church in their utmost beauty of ritual and setting. It was but natural that the various churches of Florence should vie with one another for the excellence of their choirs and the accomplishment of their organists, and, from all accounts, it seems that a really high standard of music was maintained in the various parishes. San Lorenzo and Santa Maria del Fiore were especially famous, and crowds from far and near flocked to hear the great organist of the Cathedral, Antonio Squarcialupi, whom we have to thank for the most important collection of the *Ars Nova* songs. For years he was considered one of the foremost musicians of Italy, and when he died in 1436, Lorenzo dei Medici, his patron and intimate friend, wrote the following epitaph on his tomb in the Duomo:

> Faremo insieme O Musica lamento
> Sopra il viro immortale oggi sepolto
> Morte si scusa e dice 'io ve l'ho tolto
> Per far più lieto il ciel con suo concento.

With the accession of Lorenzo il Magnifico to power, a golden age began for the artists of Florence, and, indeed, of Europe, and from all parts they flocked to the Court of this truly magnificent patron. In the palace of Via Larga or the Villas of Fiesole and Careggi, painters, poets, sculptors, musicians, philosophers, and statesmen were freely welcomed, and there they found the 'Bel Viver Italiano' of the Quattrocento in its most refined and charming aspect. They found, too, in Lorenzo an ideal host, and no political troubles or cares ever lessened his keen enjoyment of every artistic interest. He was himself a poet and musician of no mean order, and as Macchiavelli said, 'marvellously loved everything that was excellent in any art'. He was the intensely vital centre of, perhaps, the most vital and creative circle of men ever gathered together in one place since the days of Athens. Music was regarded as an absolute necessity of civilized life, and Lorenzo did his best to encourage it. He established a

School for Harmony, which was really a miniature Philharmonic Society, and many foreign musicians found their way to Florence, including a German, Heinrich Isaak, who remained there for years as Court Musician, under the name of Arrigo Tedesco. He was especially useful to Lorenzo in setting many of his verses to music, and particularly some of the Carnival songs, in which the grosser side of Lorenzo's fancy found free play. The Carnival had always appealed to the rollicking jovial strain in the Florentine nature, and before the great Frate set the torch to the Bonfire of Vanities it was indulged in whole-heartedly by every class of the people. There were processions of mummers, masquerades, and sorely distorted mystery plays, from which the sacred character had almost vanished. The old gods of Greece danced in the streets, and the Carnival songs were everywhere heard. They became, indeed, quite an important form of composition, and under Lorenzo's rule they had an immense vogue.

No time or surroundings could well have been more favourable to the development of secular music than the Court of Florence at this period, and again we cannot afford to forget that the chief source of all secular musical art is to be found in the natural desire for enjoyment. The whole fundamental conception of chamber music, for instance, rests on a social basis, and secular music during the Renaissance grew, not so much from an intellectual impulse, but rather to meet the ever increasing demands of worldly life.

Now the forms of organized entertainment can never alter much. Singing, dancing and acting may have very different settings, but they always remain the chief attractions of most festivities. All three were immensely popular in Florence. There were simple rounds and intricate dances, each with its appropriate music, when the lute and viole would be called upon for accompaniment. There were sacred *laudi* which were sung in the churches and hummed in the streets, often to popular secular airs; there were songs of every description, whether gay, or melancholy, satirical, sentimental or passionate. There were, above all, the madrigals, the most important, the most aristocratic of any song form. All the others, *canzoni*, *frottole* and their companions, had had, more or less, a popular origin, but the madrigal was the direct descendant of the *Ars Nova* songs.

It was written for two, three, four, five or more voices, sometimes accompanied by the lute, and it represents the chamber music of the fifteenth and sixteenth centuries. The madrigal literature is wonderfully rich, for it was to Italy what the chanson was to France, and many of these compositions are of great beauty. The technique of the madrigals was as finished and intricate as that of the motet, and it surely speaks highly for the general musical culture of that time that so many people must have been found able and willing to sing them. The madrigal was the musical equivalent for the verses of Petrarch and all the favourite poets, and naturally presented a great variety of emotion, sentiment, and humour. It was often a most elaborate composition, and the greatest musicians did not despise it. Cipriano da Rore, Orlando di Lasso, Festa, Palestrina, Ancrio, Animuccia, Marenzio, Gabrieli, all the great choral composers, in fact, wrote quantities of madrigals to satisfy the ever increasing demand for secular music.

With songs, dances, madrigals, poems, long discussions on Platonic philosophy and love, thus did Lorenzo and his friends pass the long summer evenings, when it was so pleasant to sit out on a Tuscan terrace beneath the stars. Marsilio Ficino, Luigi Pulci, Angiolo Poliziano and Pico della Mirandola, that most romantic of Renaissance philosophers, were among the audience which listened to the *virtuosi* and singers and criticized the latest compositions. One day, by way of novelty, perhaps, Angiolo Poliziano produced a new play he had written and had set to music, to amuse Lorenzo's guests.

Only a little more than a century earlier, Boccaccio had sung on the Fiesole hillside of the love of the streams Affrico and Mensola, and of the nymphs and spirits who haunted their glens; but to the scholars and artists who gathered at the Badia such a subject would have appeared far too insignificant; and Poliziano, true Hellenist that he was, sought for inspiration among the gods of Greece. It is almost needless to say that he chose the story of Orpheus, that most musical of myths, which has fascinated so many composers. The music, unluckily, has been lost; but the verses remain, half classic, half pastoral; and the little drama was but the first of many, the germ of something new, which, through many struggles and vicissitudes, became the music drama.

Angiolo Poliziano was tutor to Lorenzo's children, and some of the little Piero's letters to his father shed the happiest light upon the family life of Casa Medici. Education was recognized as being a matter of great importance. Religion, politics, physical training and sports, philosophy and learning of every kind had to contribute to the making of Macchiavelli's ideal 'Prince', and Poliziano often found it difficult to reconcile his ideas of the education of his charges with those of Clarice Orsini, Lorenzo's rather narrow-minded wife. He was a convinced Platonist and humanist, and with that movement there had developed the quite definite humanist educator, with different views from the masters of a former generation. The breath of the New Learning had quickly spread to other cities besides Florence, and one of the first to accept it had been Ferrara.

The position of the Este family was totally different from that of the Medici. They were not merchants, but feudal lords, and at the beginning of the fifteenth century Niccolò was already the twelfth marquess of the house of Este, nominally a vassal of the Pope, in reality absolute master of his dominions. Ferrara had been the scene of some of the darkest medieval crimes, and it had not had an artistic and literary Trecento such as Florence. Nevertheless, the Revival of

Learning made itself felt there as elsewhere, and a new epoch in Ferrarese history opens in 1429, when Niccolò looked round for a tutor to train his son Leonello as perfectly in letters as he had already been in arms. His choice fell upon Guarino, a pupil of Chrysoloras, a friend of all the Florentine humanists, and he was appointed professor of Greek and Latin at the Studium of Ferrara. Guarino's idea of education can be studied in his treatise, *De ordine docendi et Studendi*, and in it he follows the lines of all the other great humanist teachers, Poliziano, Æneas Sylvius Piccolomini (afterwards the famous humanist Pope Pius II), Vegerius and Vittorino da Feltre.

Humanist education under these masters was wonderfully complete. It looked upon the child as a complex and complete individual, needing to have each side of his nature trained and developed into an harmonious whole personality. Learning was, therefore, extremely varied, but it was never pursued for its own sake, but to build up good, and, if possible, great citizens. All the liberal arts were allowed; history and philosophy were studied from the classical authors, morals from the Fathers of the Church, recreation, gymnastics and games were encouraged. In regard to music, the humanists, as we have already seen in Florence, were divided, realizing its ideal possibilities, fearing it as a practical danger likely to have an enervating effect on the character. Saint Augustine had written warmly praising the art of music, and his words counted for much in the humanist school. The bard in Greece was a messenger of the gods, and even the Spartans allowed singing; and was not 'long-haired Iopas with his golden lyre' celebrated by Virgil?

Æneas Sylvius wrote of music: 'We must ask ourselves whether we are to include music amongst pursuits unsuited to a Prince. The Romans of the later age seem to have deprecated attention to this art in their Emperors. It was, on the other hand, held a marked defect in Themistocles that he could not tune the lyre. The armies of Lacedæmon marched to victory under the inspiration of song, and Lycurgus could not have admitted the practice had it seemed to him unworthy of the sternest manhood. The Hebrew poet king need but be alluded to, and Cicero is on his side also. So amidst some diversity of opinion, our judgement leads to the inclusion of music, as a subject to be pursued in moderation under instruction only of a serious master, who will rigorously disallow all melodies of a sensuous nature. Under these conditions we may accept the Pythagorean opinion that music exerts a soothing and refreshing influence on the mind.'

Or, again, Vegerius, in *De Ingenio Moribus:* 'As to music, the Greeks refused the title of educated to anyone unable to play or sing. Socrates set an example to the Athenian youth by himself learning to play in his old age, urging the pursuit of music, not as a sensuous indulgence, but as an aid to the inner harmony of the soul. In so far as it is taught as a healthy recreation for the moral and spiritual nature, music is a truly liberal art, and, both as regards its theory and practice, should find a place in education.'

Another note, this time of Christian philosophy, is struck by Leonardo Bruni d' Arezzo, in the letter which he wrote on education to Battista Malatesta: 'Have we not often felt the sudden uplifting of the soul when in the solemn office of the Mass such a passage as the *Primo dierum omnium* bursts upon us? It is not hard for us then to understand what the Ancients meant when they said that the soul was ordered in special relation to the principles of Harmony and Rhythm, and is, therefore, by no other influence so fitly and surely moved.'

Such was also Guarino's own attitude, and Leonello and his fellow scholars enjoyed all that the Revival of Learning could offer in education. Leonello was an apt pupil and eagerly drank in all his master could teach, and when he succeeded his father he was a 'true humanist on the throne'. Poets, men of letters, and artists flocked to Ferrara very much as they did to Florence, and Leonello himself was a poet and scholar of a high order. He was greatly attached to Guarino, who remained his lifelong friend and shared all his artistic and literary interests. These were also thoroughly congenial to Leonello's first wife, Margherita Gonzaga, brought up in the school of Vittorino da Feltre, and whose marriage was the first of the Este-Gonzaga alliances which brought the two Courts so close together. Leonello was an ardent lover of music, and he built a beautiful private chapel in the Palace, where Mass and Vespers were sung daily by a special choir he had brought to Ferrara from France. One of his chief cares was the 'Studium', and, by organizing the best lectures possible, he hoped to attract all the promising young men of his State, and to 'put to flight the clouds of ignorance and infuse the light of wisdom into the minds of his citizens'. Leonello's whole attitude to life never betrayed Guarino's teaching, and his rule was a civilizing and enlightened attempt to bring the advantage of humanist education and learning within the reach of all, and to make it an active factor in the life of the individual and of the State.

It was an age of gold for Ferrara, which reached its height in the reign of Leonello's brother Borso, who from merely Marquess of Este became a Duke of the Empire. Frederick, King of the Romans, came to Italy in 1452 for his own imperial coronation, and, with much gorgeous ceremony and lavish rejoicings, declared Borso Duke of Ferrara, Modena and Reggio, Count of Rovigo, a Prince of the Empire, one of the greatest lords of Italy.

Æneas Sylvius Piccolomini spoke in honour of the occasion. *Te Deums* were sung in the churches, there was dancing, singing and feasting in the squares, and the new Duke began a triumphal progress through his dominions with all the pomp he loved. Borso was a very popular ruler. His good looks and genial manner endeared him to all, while his liberality and generosity became proverbial throughout Europe. He was a man of peace, and politically steered wisely through many storms. Though he could not boast of any particular intellectual culture, he continued all Leonello's patronage of art and learning. Ferrara, so far, had not produced any first-rate local painters, though many of the best Italian masters had worked there, but now the genuine Ferrarese school shone with artists such as Cosimo Tura and Francesco del Cossa. Borso's life ended amidst the glitter of his Court and the genuine affection of many of his subjects, and all this splendour fell to the share of his brother, the new Duke Ercole I.

He was the typical Italian despot, magnificent in peace and war, with all his brother's love of display, a great ruler, and a liberal patron of science and art. Endless gorgeous pageants fill the pages of Ferrarese history, one of the first being for his own wedding with Leonora of Aragon. She made a triumphal progress from Naples, was received in Rome by the Pope with every possible honour, lodged in Florence with all her retinue in the Medici Palace, with the young Lorenzo and Giuliano to wait on her at meals, and what matter if some of the careful Florentines did grumble at the waste of public money in such lavish hospitality! Leonora was received in her husband's dominions with 'stupendissimo onore', and in all her subsequent life she showed herself well worthy of the honours so generously showered upon her.

All and any excuse for festivities were welcome to Ercole, if it gave him the opportunity to indulge his passion for the stage. In 1486 he inaugurated a series of theatrical performances in Ferrara which, according to Professore d'Ancona, were the direct cause of the rise of the secular drama in contradistinction to the old mystery plays and *Sacra Rappresentazione*. Terence and Plautus were perpetually performed with the most elaborate settings, and Ercole proudly showed his guests the hundred and ten different dresses which were used in five comedies of Plautus. All Ferrara was stage-struck, and the Duke was constantly demanding new plays or dramatic poems. Of these there was no lack. Ercole's Court shone with the lustre of many poets, Tito Vespasiano di Messer Nanni Strozzi, Tebaldeo, Cammelli, Niccolò Correggio, all men of talent, and, most eminent of all, Matteo Maria Boiardo, whose *Orlando Innamorato* is the Arthurian legend and romance in a fanciful Italian dress. Into this *milieu* came the young Ludovico Ariosto, the poet grand seigneur, who is one of the shining lights of Italian literature and so well deserved the title Prof. Gardner has given him, 'the King of Court Poets'.

In all this music played an important part. The Duke of Ferrara was famous for his private orchestra, which included lutes, viols, lyres, cembalo, cornets, trombones, zampogna and organ, and the best-known performers were secured at a high salary. A good musician of the Renaissance had, indeed, every chance of making his way. Once he had secured the favour of a music-loving prince, all was then well, for he became a regular member of the Court, and Ercole I was a much-sought-after patron. His choir was renowned throughout Italy, and in it were Italian, French, and Spanish singers.

To Ferrara also came many of the Flemish composers, Hobrecht, Brumel, Josquin, and others, and they found a never-failing welcome, and splendid facilities for the performance of their works.

Later on, Cipriano da Rore was choirmaster to Ercole II, and Luzzaschi organist in Ferrara, whilst Marenzio, the greatest of all madrigal composers, 'dolce cigno, divin compositore', as he was called, was in the service of the Cardinale d' Este. The musical life in Ferrara did not flag for another hundred years or so, and many of the great musicians of Northern Italy sought an appointment there.

The Castle of Ferrara was not only a brilliant Court but a happy home, and Ercole and the Duchess Leonora's two daughters, Isabella and Beatrice, were queens of the Renaissance. They were educated with their brothers Alfonso and Ferrante in the school of Guarino, for the wonderful little girls of the Quattro- and Cinquecento were, indeed, learned in a way that later generations quite lost sight of. The Este princesses were beautiful and charming and accomplished: they could write Latin verse and knew the classics well; they sang and played the lute and other instruments, they embroidered, they hunted, they danced, they improvised, they learnt to perfection the art of life. Fortunately for us they were also great letter-writers, and we can follow them and their friends in all their daily lives. Naturally Ercole sought brilliant marriages for his daughters, and Isabella was betrothed to Federigo Gonzaga, son of the

Marquess of Mantua, and Beatrice to Ludovico Sforza, 'Il Moro', the Regent of Milan. The future must, indeed, have looked golden to these two girls, surrounded as they were by all the beauty and luxury and culture of their father's Court; themselves the centre of so much love and admiration, receiving the adulation of poets as their due, conscious of their own power.

When the time came for the wedding festivities, artists and goldsmiths, able craftsmen of every kind, were kept busy making presents for the brides: gold and silver plate, tapestries, singers, and musicians were all freely borrowed from other Courts for the great occasion. Isabella was married in Ferrara in 1490, and after the gorgeous ceremonies she left her old home in a gilded barge with ambassadors from every State in Italy in the attendant galleys, to be welcomed to a city hung with banners and garlanded with flowers, with all Mantua gathered to do honour to the young Marquess and his bride.

Beatrice's wedding was, if possible, even more brilliant. She was escorted to Milan by her mother, sister, and brother Alfonso, who was to fetch away his own bride, Anna Sforza. The accounts of her wedding and triumphant entry into Milan seem to bring the most glittering of Renaissance pictures to life before our eyes. The marvellous dresses, the pageants and tournaments, were all on a scale of unheard-of magnificence: a hundred trumpeters welcomed Beatrice, choirs sang her praises, and Leonardo da Vinci, the Milanese

Court Painter, thought it in no wise beneath his dignity to design and direct one of the masquerades given in her honour.

It was a triumph of all this world could offer: riches, beauty, power. Life seemed to give with both hands to her who was to enjoy it all for so short a time, whilst for 'Il Moro' was reserved the more bitter doom of exile, degradation and a languishing death in a foreign prison. Surely there he must often have echoed the words of that other Renaissance Prince, Lorenzo il Magnifico, 'Fallace vita, O nostra vana cura', when he looked back to life in Milan, and himself one of the great rulers of Italy!

V

MUSIC AT THE COURTS OF ITALY (*continued*)

Mantua and Urbino

The man that hath no music in himself
Nor is not moved with concord of sweet sounds,
Is fit for treasons, stratagems and spoils . . . .

Merchant of Venice

La musica . . . chi non la gusta si può tener certo che abbia gli spiriti discordanti l' un dall' altro . . . .

Count Baldassare Castiglione

The Italy of Shakespeare! What a magic country, it is full of the enchantment and glamour of a fairy tale, and, somehow, it is in Mantua that we seem to come nearest to it. The halls of the Gonzagas are empty, their treasures long since dispersed and gone to enrich half the galleries of Europe. Giulio Romano's Palazzo del Té and Isabella d' Este's Paradiso are silent, and terribly desolate, but as one looks out of her windows over the lakes to her 'heavenly view', or wanders through the rooms decorated by Mantegna, the fantastic charm of the place wafts one irresistibly back to the days of its glory, to the Mantua that Shakespeare knew, to the people whose ideas he shared.

'This most sweet Paradise, this *domicilium Venerum et Charitum* . . . this is the citie wich of all other places in the world I would wish.' That was how Mantua struck the English traveller Coryat, who published a guide to Italy in 1611, and it was chiefly around Isabella d' Este and her son that the poets and artists had gathered who made Mantua worthy of her name, *La Gloriosa.*

When Isabella married, she found at her husband's Court a society every whit as brilliant and accomplished as the one she had left in Ferrara. The Gonzagas were amongst the greatest people of Italy, and politically were of European importance. The Marchese Francesco's grandfather, Ludovico, had been brought up under Vittorino da Feltre, the eminent humanist schoolmaster. It was, indeed, fitting that Mantua, the birthplace of Virgil, should be the home of the first modern school, and the boys at La Gioiosa had a first-rate education.

Vittorino was a friend of Guarino's, and seems to have been bent, first of all, on setting a high standard of faith and conduct before the boys, and then to train their minds according to the traditions of classical learning, and to develop their bodies by healthy sports and games.

His view of music was that of the other humanists, and carefully chosen masters gave lessons to those boys and girls who showed any marked talent. Musical education in those days was very different to what it is now. The *virtuoso* element which set musicians as a class apart was much less insisted upon, but, in order to take one's place in ordinary cultivated society, almost every one was expected to sing a melody at sight and improvise the accompaniment, and that in itself meant a high degree of musical accomplishment. Vittorino's whole character commanded the love and respect of those under him, and the condition he made before accepting the invitation of Gianfrancesco Gonzaga was typical of him. His words to the Marquess are reported as having been: 'I accept the post on this understanding only, that you require nothing which shall be in any way unworthy of either of us, and I will continue to serve you so long as your own life shall command respect.'

Ludovico showed himself the worthy pupil of such a master. He was greater in peace than in war, and his dominions prospered throughout his reign. It was he who commissioned Giovan Battista Alberti to build the Cathedral of Sant' Andrea, which was followed by the Palazzo Belvedere and the Hospital, and he was the first generous patron of the young Andrea Mantegna. By his order a printing-press was set up, and he welcomed writers and poets from the other Italian States. The works of Petrarch and all the Florentine poets met with great success in Mantua, and no sooner had the news of Poliziano's *Orfeo* spread north, than he received an invitation to superintend its performance at the Gonzaga Court.

Vittorino had died in 1446, but the tradition of his teaching remained, and Isabella's husband, Francesco, had received much the same education as his wife. He was the real *condottiere* in war, an out-of-doors man, loving his horses and dogs, but proud of the artistic refinement of his home life, and, above all, proud of the brilliant centre of his Court, the Marchesa Isabella.

The *Prima Donna del Mondo*, as she was called, has the fascination for us that we can know her at first hand. More than two thousand of her letters exist to show her to us in every detail of life. And how well they are written! We do not need to read about her. Here she is herself, with her brilliant intellectual gifts, discussing literature, philosophy, or the arts; devouring every new book, excited over new songs and music, or cautiously advising her husband in some difficult political move. We feel her charm, her tact, her kindness. And how human she is with her foibles and little vanities, and the despair over her dog's death! She lives wholeheartedly and intensely in the joy or sorrow of the moment, and her natural shrewdness generally leads her to make the best of every situation. She is full of love for her husband, her children, her sister Beatrice, all her family, in fact, and especially for her sister-in-law Elisabetta, wife of Guidobaldo Duke of Urbino. 'There is no one I love like you, except my sister Beatrice', she wrote to her, and the passing years only strengthened this tender affection.

The first years of the Este sisters' married lives saw a perpetual intercourse between the Courts of Ferrara, Mantua, and Milan. Poets and musicians were handed on from one to the other; life was often troubled, and yet how gay, how interesting and, above all, how full they made it! Isabella and Beatrice were talked of by all the fashionable society of Europe, their entertainments and clothes were eagerly discussed, they were the cynosure of all eyes. The greatest artists painted them, Ariosto, Boiardo, Niccolò Correggio, and many a lesser poet sang their praises, and they lived in an atmosphere of perpetual adulation. True daughters of the Renaissance, they had its beauty and graces without its cruelty, its refinement without its vices, and they lived for this world, in the best spirit of their age.

Isabella especially was of an acquisitive nature, and showed the real characteristics of the born art collector. She delighted in the work of decorating her apartments in the Palace, or planning a new villa and garden. Pictures, statues, tapestries, beautiful furniture and *objets d'art*, were all seized on to satisfy her taste; if she heard of some lovely or valuable thing, instantly she had to have it, or at least to write long letters to try to get it. The decorative sense of the Cinquecento was so strong that every object had to be beautiful, and musical instruments as pleasing to the eye as their sound was sweet to the ear. Isabella possessed harps, lutes, and clavichords on which the most delicate workmanship had been lavished, and she devotes one long letter to describing the details of an inlaid lute for which she longed. Leonardo da Vinci had first been received in Milan, not for his genius as a painter, but on account of a 'silver' lute, shaped like a horse's head, that he had brought from Florence for the Duke's inspection. Leonardo was himself an accomplished musician, and either he or his friend, the composer Gafurio, who spent a couple of years in Mantua, wrote the music for the *Paradiso*, a musical 'commedia' with the words by Bellincioni, which Leonardo had produced in Milan for the wedding of Galeazzo Sforza and Isabella degli Aragonesi di Napoli. We may be sure that Isabella d' Este had heard all about it, and that Leonardo was called upon to help her, at least with his advice, in the theatrical performances of the Mantuan Court. It was probably Leonardo who told her of the splendid organ that his friend Lorenzo di Pavia was making for Leo X, almost as insatiable a collector as Isabella herself. Then an alabaster one is mentioned, which was made for the Pope in Naples, and was said to be unsurpassed for its workmanship and beauty of tone. This, Isabella was determined to get, and her chance came when Pope Leo died, and, after a certain amount of haggling, she managed to secure it for six hundred ducats.

Music in Mantua was a much cultivated art. Excellent *virtuosi* were attached to the Court, and a contemporary account mentions the viole, lute, lyre, cembalo, cornet, trombone, zampogna and organ as being 'some of the instruments that anyone of good education should know how to play'. But then who can look at the standard of learning and accomplishments in the men and women of the Renaissance, and not be filled with amazement and respect?

'Concert' is too abused a word for the musical gatherings of such a circle as the Gonzagas, where music was unhampered by the set routine of the *virtuoso* programme, and the audience was in real contact with the performer, and could follow each delicate phrase or shade of tone. Thus, and thus only, indeed, can music of an intimate character, real 'chamber music', truly live, for so much of its effect must always depend on the sympathy and perception of the listeners.

Isabella and her companions were themselves good performers: they sang all the latest madrigals and songs, played all the lute and viole music they could find, and they knew, too, how to be an excellent audience. The Gonzaga choir was famous, and in after years Isabella's son was the friend of Palestrina.

Men like Continuo and Porta came to Mantua as choir-masters, and Porta's great pupil Viadana was born near by and succeeded his master as Cathedral organist. There Salomone Rossi the Rabbi wrote his famous sonatas, which rivalled Gabrieli's and were amongst the first formal instrumental compositions. Alessandro Striggio was also born in Mantua and, though he went to Florence and was a renowned composer of interlude music at the Court of Cosimo I, he returned home after some years, bringing to Mantua the ideas of Peri and Caccini and the Florentine Reform.

The Mantuan Alberto Ripi was the chief lute player at the Court of François I, and composed a quantity of charming lute music, and an interesting account of musical life in

Mantua is given by the poet Teofilo Folengo in his *Maccaroneide*. It contains a comic description of a quartet and an amusing parody of musical fanaticism. Italian, French, and Spanish songs and singing were the fashion, and especially the works of Josquin de Près and all the Flemish school. Folengo, indeed, probably knew these well, and it is even possible that Josquin and Hobrecht, during their stay in Ferrara, also visited Mantua.

Mantua was one of the most musical cities of Italy, and many of the Venetian and Lombard musicians were well known there. The composer could be sure his works would be well performed and listened to by a sympathetic and understanding public. It was in Mantua that Monteverde first showed his striking genius, and the Gonzagas were the first patrons of his dramatic works.

Music was a delightful social pastime to Isabella and the friends she found in both Mantua and Milan. Here gathered Leonardo, Calmeta, Cristoforo Romano (equally gifted as sculptor and singer), the Neapolitan musician Muzio Effren, Testagrossa, Tromboncino, Jacopo di San Secondo (Beatrice's favourite lute player), and, above all, Baldassare di Castiglione, who was related to the Gonzaga family.

To few men is it given to be the hero of their own book, but Castiglione was the perfect courtier, the living example of all he described in the *Cortigiano*, not only, as he has been called, the Italian Lord Chesterfield, but also, surely, the Italian Sir Philip Sidney. In that age of universal men, when no talents were left uncultivated which could add to the grace and splendour of mere human existence, Castiglione shines out as that human work of art of the Renaissance, the perfect man of Society. This, however, not in any trivial way, for Castiglione distinguished himself not only as lover and friend, scholar and poet, but also as an extremely able diplomat and statesman. After Beatrice's death and the *débâcle* in Milan, Isabella clung more than ever to him and to her beloved Elisabetta, and the scene moves from Milan and Mantua to Urbino.

If Isabella was the more brilliant, Elisabetta was, perhaps, the most noble and attractive of all the Renaissance ladies, and how clearly the difference in their characters can be seen in their respective portraits by Titian and Mantegna! In the same way, Mantua may have been the most gorgeous, but Urbino was undoubtedly the most romantic of Renaissance cities. 'The men of Urbino were pre-eminent in all sorts of principal arts, an honour to their predecessors, an example to posterity', says one inscription; and amongst them were Rafaello and Bramante, and that greatest ruler of the Italian Quattrocento, Duke Federigo di Montefeltro, whose portrait, with his wife, Battista Sforza, by Piero della Francesca, meets us in the Uffizi Gallery in Florence.

'It is well known,' writes Ruscelli in his *Impressi Illustri*, 'and beyond any contradicting, that the house of Urbino and della Rovere for a long time past has been illustrious in Italy, in letters, in arms and in every rare virtue', and Federigo di

Montefeltro was a shining example of the qualities of his race. Poliziano praised him as the equal of Lorenzo as a patron of the arts, and Marsilio Ficino as a 'perfect man'. He had been a fellow pupil of Ludovico Gonzaga under Vittorino da Feltre, and the Court of Urbino was modelled on the ideas of *La Gioiosa*. Federigo transformed the grim fortress, by the help of Luciano da Laurana, into what was surely one of the most beautiful dwelling-houses ever planned. It was enormous, a perfect house, perfectly kept by an army of servants. Even to-day, shorn of its treasures and its wonderful library, the beauty of the rooms and decorations still show what it must have been in the days of its splendour. Duke Federigo was a father to his people, he cared for them in every way, and his wise and kind rule brought unwonted prosperity to his State.

As a patron of learning he was most enlightened, and made a magnificent collection of books, manuscripts, musical scores, and instruments. A favourite organ was built for him by Johanno Castellano, and his own study was decorated with a frieze of musical instruments. Vespasiano di Besticci, the Florentine biobliophile, wrote of the Duke: 'He always had great pleasure in music and thoroughly understood both vocal and instrumental composition. He had a choir composed of excellent musicians, boys singing treble, and tenors. There was no instrument that His Lordship had not in his house, and he greatly enjoyed their sound and had in his palace perfect instrumental players. He preferred smaller instruments to larger ones, trumpets and instruments of that kind he did not care for, but all smaller ones and the organ he greatly loved.'

Guidobaldo, his son, inherited all Federigo's love of music, and had an excellent music master in Ottaviano de' Petrucci di Fossombrone. When he married Elisabetta Gonzaga he found in his wife a companion who shared all his artistic and intellectual tastes, and in their wonderful castle he and the Mantuan princess gathered round them a delightful circle of congenial spirits. There were the charming Emilia Pia (inseparable friend of the Duchess), the Cardinals Bembo and Bibbiena, Ottaviano and Federico Fregoso, Tebaldeo (who had been Isabella's master in the art of verse), Giuliano dei Medici (afterwards to become, through marriage, Duc de Nemours), Calmeta, Canossa, Cristoforo Romano, and Castiglione. Every one who knew Elisabetta loved her, and Castiglione, with his genius for friendship, offered her the devotion of his whole life. Many poets, including Tasso, praised her, and Bembo wrote: 'I have seen many excellent and noble women, and have known some who were conspicuous for certain virtues in their time, but in her alone all virtues were summed up. I have never seen or heard of anyone who was her equal, and know very few who have even come near her.' She was great both in prosperity and adversity, and may well have been a model for her husband's little niece, Vittoria Colonna.

Many great artists came to Urbino in those years to paint,

and the Duke was particularly interested in the local painter, Giovanni Santi, and afterwards in his orphan son Rafaello, who immortalized so many of the Urbino Court in his *Stanze* of the Vatican. Musicians, too, there were in numbers. Jacopo di San Secondo (the Apollo of Rafaello's *Parnassus*), Barletta (the favourite musician of Elisabetta, 'a most pleasing musician and excellent dancer, who always kept the whole Court in *festa*'), Bernardino, d' Urbino, Adriano (poet, sculptor and musician), Serafino Ciminelli dell' Aquila, Gaspare Siciliano, Testagrossa, Gian Maria Gaudio, Terpandro, and the Lord Morello da Ortona, fine lute-players all of them, and, greatest of all, Marchetto Cara, who for years had been in the service of the Marquess of Mantua. He was an excellent singer and composer, lent to the Court of Urbino by Isabella; his songs and madrigals were widely known, and some of them were published in the Petrucci Collection. Besides these visitors there were naturally the singers of the Ducal choir and the regular musicians of the Court, kept on as in Duke Federigo's days.

News of the splendour of Urbino, we may be sure, travelled quickly back to Mantua, and it was not long before Isabella and her husband went there for a visit. She acknowledged that her expectations had been surpassed, and that even her Paradiso was less perfect than the Montefeltro Palace. Then there was the joy of being with Elisabetta, and of Guidobaldo she wrote: 'He holds a fine Court here and lives in royal splendour, and governs the State with great wisdom and humanity to the satisfaction of all his subjects.'

Unluckily he was often ill, and much time was spent in reading, music, and impromptu plays and recitations to distract him. It is Castiglione, in his matchless book of the *Cortigiano*, who has opened for us this enchanting society of the Montefeltros and Gonzagas. When those years were but a golden memory he wished to revive them, to leave a picture of what the Court of Urbino had been, and seldom, surely, has a writer succeeded so completely in capturing in cold print the evanescent charm of the moment. We feel the fascination of those friends in their affectionate familiarity and ease, where each understood the other so well that a word or gesture or 'flash of silence' was enough to explain their meaning: 'At Urbino the discussions were broken by hunting, riding and hawking parties, by dance and music; but all was refined by wit and intellect. In summer, the brilliant gathering would often be held in the fair gardens, on a grassy lawn, under shady trees, sheltered from sun and wind. At other times the meeting would have a splendid setting—in a fair palace hall with hangings of silk and tapestry, or of rich cloth of gold adorned with a wonderful number of rare antiques in marble and bronze, most excellent paintings, and instruments of music. . . . When the evening came, the company assembled where the Duchess was with her ladies, each sitting at his will in a circle as it always chanced . . . and she was the chain which kept all linked harmoniously in pleasant converse, subtle imagination and witty jests.'

Here they discussed every question of philosophy and art, they laughed and told stories, with what quick humour, delicate irony and sympathy! Castiglione himself had travelled, it was he who went to England, to stand proxy for Guidobaldo when Henry VII conferred the Garter on him, and Castiglione knew the leading figures of the English Court, and was in touch with English life. He and all the Urbino circle were essentially cosmopolitan in spirit. 'What should be the chief virtues of the perfect courtier?' asked Monsignore Federico Fregoso one evening, and Conte Lodovico di Canossa answered, describing every accomplishment of birth and education, every manly sport and game, including tennis, 'which requires such great quickness and nimbleness', the science of war and arms, the graces of learning, and, above all, that 'crown of art, which is to hide all art, and make it seem like nature'. 'The courtier must be a musician and should have skill on sundry instruments', and when some one objected that such delicate occupation would make him effeminate and weak, 'Speak it not,' cried the Count Lodovico, 'for I would give high praise to music, which has always been renowned. Wise philosophers say the world is made of music, and that the Heavens, in their moving, make a melody. Socrates played the harp, stern Lycurgus permitted music, great Achilles learnt it of Charon, and many great men and warriors loved it well. We see it used in holy temples to laud and praise God, while labouring folk beguile their toil with song, and prisoners in adversity, and babes are hushed to sleep by it. Music is the charm of life, its light, its sunny grace; no art responds thus to the needs of our nature, none brings us such various and vivid emotions. It calms and penetrates us and raises us to Heaven with the quick beating of its wings.'

Never has music been better praised, and, as the book nears its end, Castiglione puts into Bembo's mouth a hymn to love and beauty, in which is expressed the quintessence of all that was finest in Renaissance neo-platonism: 'Love is the desire for beauty, and spiritual love is the soul's desire for ideal beauty. . . . And this is Love. . . . the infusion of Divine Beauty shining on all the created world. . . . Let us, therefore, turn to this sacred light which shows us the path to Heaven; let us climb the steep steps to the high place where beauty dwells, and there we shall find a happy rest, and a safe refuge in the troublous storms and the tempestuous sea of life. What mortal tongue can worthily praise Thee, oh most holy Love? Thou, most beautiful, most good, most wise. From the union of divine goodness and beauty and wisdom, Thou dost come forth and to it Thou dost return. Thou art the sweetest bond of union in this world. . . . Thou dost harmonize the elements, move Nature to produce all that is born in the succession of life. Thou dost unite that which is separate, takest away all imperfection, turning foes to friends. Thou givest to the earth her fruits, to the sea its calm, to the sky its life-giving light. Lord, hear this our prayer, come into our hearts, and as a sure guide show us the path in this dark labyrinth. . . . Make us to hear the celestial harmony and concord that all the discord of our passions may be stilled. . . . With the bright rays of Thy Light cleanse our eyes from the mists of ignorance, that they may no longer seek for mortal beauty. Accept our souls which we offer Thee and burn them in that fire which consumes that which is hideous and material, and with the most sweet and lasting bond we may be united to the Divine Beauty and be admitted to the feast of the angels on high . . . .'

So long did this discussion last, and so entranced were the listeners, that 'When the windows were thrown open on that side of the Palace which looks towards the heights of Monte Catari, they saw that the east was aglow with the rosy dawn, and the stars had faded, save only Venus, the sweet ruler of the sky, who keeps the bounds of day and night. Then there came a soft breeze which awoke the song of birds in the wooded groves of the hill-side. Whereupon they all took leave with reverence of the Duchess and departed homewards without torches, the light of day sufficing.'

Amidst such rapturous discourse Castiglione and his friends turned to our poor mortal music with obvious pleasure. Sometimes there would be singing, and they delighted in the music of the Flemish composers; indeed, Josquin's setting of Virgil's 'Lament for Dido' was Elisabetta's favourite song. Or they might wish for an instrumental quartet: lutes, viols, clavichords, or an organ composition, or some new music of Marchetto Cara's. If the company preferred, there was Fra Serafino, or else *l' Unico Aretino*, as he was affectionately called, ready to improvise to the lute. His written verse probably gives no idea of his ready wit and power of improvisation, which was so great that it was said that on his arrival in a place even the shops were shut, so strong was the general wish to hear him.

To those who have had the good fortune to hear Italian *improvisatori* this sounds in no way unlikely. Alas! they are now rare, but not many years ago the public story-tellers round Florence were delightful, and still in the more remote districts, the mountains of the Abruzzi, or village fairs in the South, the *improvisatore* is to be heard, amazing in his flow of wit, and imagination, and beauty of language.

From singing, playing, and improvising, what could be more pleasant than to end an evening with dancing? And four pipers especially skilled in such music had come from Ferrara. There would be dances, grave and gay, and often accompanied by songs. Most intricate was the *moresca*, which had journeyed to Italy by way of Spain and Naples from the East. It was essentially dramatic: a succession of scenes and dances, with singing and recitations, and could be drawn out to fill a whole evening. It was more often used as an *intermezzo* in some larger performance, such as Castiglione's *Tirsi,* a dramatic pastoral poem, which was followed by Bembo's fine *Stanze Pastorali*, written on the model of Poliziano's *Stanze*. Each of these ended with a *moresca* in which 'figured shepherds, cavaliers and ladies, singing as they danced'. Bembo was already well known for his other poems in Italian, especially the *Asolani* (printed by the Aldine Press, and dedicated to Lucrezia Borgia), and Castiglione represented him in *Tirsi* as the 'most famous of the shepherds' come from Adria to the Court of Urbino. The most important dramatic composition of those years, however, was Bibbiena's *Calandra*, produced during the Carnival of 1513. It was a farce in Italian, more or less on the lines of Plautus, and an invisible orchestra, songs and solo instrumental pieces accompanied the play, which had the greatest success. It was afterwards performed in France at the command of Henri II, and also in Rome, Ferrara, and Mantua, where a splendid new theatre had been opened, all hung with *Trionfi* by Mantegna.

The Duke Guidobaldo of Montefeltro died in 1518, and with the scattering of the Urbino Court one of the bright lights of the Renaissance was darkened. Directly and indirectly its influence reached far beyond Italy, and how much charm our own Elizabethan literature owes to the *Book of the Courtier* and that little hill town of the Marches! Endless political difficulties and wars followed the succession of Francesco Maria della Rovere to his uncle's possessions, and Elisabetta found herself a fugitive in Mantua and elsewhere before peace was restored.

Soon after his return home, Castiglione went to Rome as Mantuan ambassador, and his letters give a vivid picture of the brilliant Court of Leo X. The drama and music were particularly beloved by this Medici Pope, and the Roman public had grown used to dramatic shows, both sacred and secular, *moresche* and *intermezzi*, one more elaborate than the other.

Evidently the Cinquecento audience really enjoyed these performances, for the Italian public has always been critical, if not cruel, and surely none other knows so well how to hiss! The fact that the *moresche*, plays, and interludes had such success proves that they were, in some ways at least, artistically pleasing, for there was no lack of critical taste at that time.

Isabella and her brothers, Duke Alfonso II of Ferrara and Cardinal Ippolito d' Este, that 'most vigorous body and fiercest mind of his house', had all the Este love of music and acting. Some of the most famous musicians, as we have already seen, were in their service, and they took a passionate interest in the drama. For Alfonso's marriage to Lucrezia Borgia there had been *commedie*, *moresche*, and symbolical pageants, and Lucrezia had introduced some new Spanish dances with her own tambourine players. On this occasion, however, Isabella and Elisabetta, who were both there, appear to have been heavily bored. Perhaps their aversion to the marriage made them less inclined to enjoy themselves, and Isabella wrote to her husband to say how far she would prefer to be at home with him and the '*puttino*,' as she calls their baby son.

In Ferrara there were perpetual *feste*, concerts, and plays, and the theatre of the Corte Vecchia was superintended by Ariosto. *Cassaria* and the *Suppositi, Negromante* and *Scolastica* were all real Italian comedies written for various carnivals and merry-makings. Alfonso's son Ercole was a poet and excellent musician like his great-uncle Leonello, and when he brought home as bride Renée, daughter of King Louis XII of France, Ferrara, indeed, did its utmost to receive her with honour.

Isabella's son Federigo, brought up partly at the resplendent Papal Court, came back to Mantua with many Roman friends. Giulio Romano was at work at the enchanting Palazzo del Tè, and Federigo had as many musicians in his household as the Cardinal Ippolito himself. There were great rejoicings in Mantua for his marriage, cleverly brought about by his mother, with Margherita Paleologa, the heiress of Monferrato, and in 1532, when Mantua prepared to receive the Emperor with much splendour, and Federigo was rewarded with the coveted title of Duke.

Life had been saddened by the death, in 1526, of Elisabetta Gonzaga. She had lived to see the duchy restored to her nephew and his wife, Isabella's daughter, and another little Guidobaldo growing up in Urbino. Her loss was an irreparable one to her family and friends, and above all to her sister-in-law. Isabella lived on till 1539, spending much time at a country villa amongst her children and treasures and flowers, and to the end she was her own brilliant self, walking successfully upon the 'sunlit high road of the Renaissance'.

VI

THE FLORENTINE REFORM

Quelle opere che si fanno agevolmente
Son poco degne, perchè presto han fine.

BENVENUTO CELLINI

THE Medici had, indeed, been wise when they took as a motto the words '*Si volge*'; and how often the wheel of fortune turned for that remarkable family! The year 1494 saw an end to all that Lorenzo had built up. Charles VIII entered Florence and the Medici were put to flight. Four years afterwards came the death of Savonarola, and foreign conquerors trampled Italy under foot. In Florence it was a glorious moment only for art, with Leonardo, Michelangelo, Andrea del Sarto, Fra Bartolomeo, Piero di Cosimo, and Filippino all at work. A change came in 1512 when, thanks to a Spanish invasion, the Medici found themselves reinstated, somewhat unsteadily, under Lorenzo, nephew to Leo X. He came back to power with none of the republican ideas of his grandfather Lorenzo il Magnifico, but full of ambition, and he saw with great satisfaction his only child Caterina married to Henri II—a brilliant alliance, indeed, for the Medici. It was not, however, till 1537 that they found themselves again firmly established in Florence, this time in the person of the despotic Cosimo I, the first Medicean Grand Duke.

Perhaps the Florentines were glad to see the return of their former masters. After the Bonfire of Vanities, on which, amongst other things, much valuable music perished, and when Savonarola's reforming presence was removed, there came a reaction, and the people took kindly enough once more to shows and pageants, feasting and amusement. There was plenty of all this, and, as might be expected, Florence was second to no city in Italy in the wealth and brilliancy of her Court functions. During the Cinque- and Seicento, there are records of a vast number of festivities, all in honour of some event connected with the Medici family. In 1539 the marriage of Cosimo I with Eleonora of Toledo (the Eleonora who looks down at us from Bronzino's portrait in the Uffizi) was made the occasion of the most sumptuous rejoicing. She entered Florence by the same historic road down which Charles VIII and many other kings had passed. Deputations met her before she reached the town, and as she came within sight of the walls the chief officers of the city gathered about the gaily decorated Porta al Prato to receive her. A band of musicians was stationed in the loggia above the gate-way, and choruses of eight voices welcomed her, as the procession rested before proceeding upon its triumphal progress through the streets. Then followed a banquet and a *Commedia*, with interludes, and nearly all the music was written by Francesco Corteccia, an excellent musician who was in the service of the Duke as choirmaster of the Church of San Lorenzo. He was a native of Arezzo, but lived for many years in Florence, and his heart seems always to have been more in his singing gallery than in the pageants of the Court, in which he was so often called upon to help.

Cosimo invited many musicians to his Court, and even Costantino Festa was induced to leave Rome for a few years and spend them in Florence in the Grand Duke's service. There were local composers, too, with plenty of talent, and in the manuscripts of the sixteenth century a quantity of attractive *ballate* and madrigals are to be found, all by Florentine musicians.

The year 1565 saw great rejoicings again, when Don Francesco dei Medici brought home Giovanna d' Austria as his bride. Even the Medici could afford to be well satisfied with such a marriage—Giovanna was rich, her family was powerful—Cosimo was proud of his son and daughter-in-law, and spared no money in making the wedding as brilliant an affair as possible. He commissioned Corteccia, Striggio, Matteo Rampolini, Moschini and Costantino Festa to write the necessary music, and there was the usual endless round of banquets, plays, interludes, and concerts.

There is an interesting account of the instruments which were used on this occasion, and they included four *gravicembali doppi*, four *violi d' arco*, two trombones, two *flauti tenore*, one *cornetto*, one *traversa*, and two lutes. What a vision of the future we see in this Cinquecento Florentine orchestra! and the great period of chamber and orchestral music dimly comes into sight. Already the *cembalo* was asserting itself as a dominant factor in concerted music. It provided the foundation, and sustained the other instruments, and for another two hundred and fifty years the composer appears seated at the first *cembalo* leading his work, conducting the concerto.

We cannot here follow in detail the many baptism and wedding festivities of Casa Medici, dazzling as they are, and full of interest and fascination. The princesses Cristina di Lorena and Maria Maddalena of Austria came to Florence to wed the descendants of the great Cosimo, while even the King of France was anxious to bind the powerful Florentine family to the French crown. Pageant followed pageant during those years of Medici prosperity, with much costly entertaining in the splendid palaces, games, banquets, dances, plays, and music. The life of society was constantly becoming more elaborate, and everything had to be on a splendid scale, but though these *feste* were often described in glowing terms, as far as the stage was concerned the artistic result was small. There were too many distracting elements, and the very wealth of scenic display only hindered any real dramatic interest. The organizers undoubtedly started with the serious wish to create an harmonious whole, very difficult at any time, and certainly impossible under the then existing conditions. Secular instrumental music was still too unformed, and the love of spectacular display too strong, for any real balance to be achieved.

There is scarcely anything written for the stage in those days which appears to us now as more enduring than a poor wooden doll whose finery has all withered away. One of the most convincing compositions of that time is the remarkable spiritual drama *Ara Beatrice*, written by the nun Suor Beatrice del Sera for the community of a Tuscan convent, and which has more the quality of a mystery play. Otherwise there is very little, for neither Plautus nor Terence, Bibbiena or the Florentine Court writers, make a genuine human appeal: Court poets, like Bellincioni or Strozzi, were generally too much bent on pleasing their patrons, or writing things to order, for their work to have any lasting interest. The truest success lay, perhaps, with the 'Comedia d' Arte', but in all larger compositions the drama must have been considerably hindered, to our ideas at least, by the interludes, mythological fables, Roman gladiators, rustic scenes: anything and everything was sandwiched in between the acts of the actual drama, which ended by becoming nothing more than a large piece of irrelevant patchwork.

Another source of weakness lay in the very fact that practically all these plays were *pièces d'occasion*, and that, therefore, the first and most important point was that they should please the patron for whom they were written. Money could be, and was, squandered upon them, but always upon the external and spectacular side of the performance. And

here, of course, we come to the real difficulty, which was that there was exceedingly little inspiration. The whole growth sprang from shallow soil, from no compelling creative impulse, and therefore, like a tropical flower, was doomed to fade quickly. Yet this was the dramatic material to which composers were to add their art, and it was certainly not promising. Music could have but little scope when the attention of the audience was almost entirely riveted on the marvellous transformations and scenic tricks which were constantly passing before their eyes.

The greatest musical talent of the Cinquecento could not compensate for the artistic weakness of the *intermezzi*, though many of the best composers wrote the music for them. The scenic action all too often obscured the real qualities of both text and music. The strength and weakness of the art of music lies in its dependence upon a powerful emotional impulse. It cannot become great if there be no well of inspiration and imagination from whence it may spring. Of this compelling quality there is practically none in the *Paradiso* and its kindred *Commedie*. As dramas they barely existed; as a succession of scenes, so loosely linked together as sometimes to appear altogether isolated, many were brilliant and fantastic, some were tender and gay, and nearly all were effective. But of any more enduring quality there was remarkably little. There was, above all, no continuity in either text or music: in spite of charming songs and instrumental pieces, these so-called dramatic performances, in which dramatic characterization hardly even existed, were never more than disjointed plays, interlarded with concerts. This was not entirely due to the shortcomings of the text, for the truth was that instrumental music was not ready for this new task: its style was yet too unformed. The Troubadours had known how to adapt Gregorian music and folk-songs to their own purposes. The Italians of the Quattro- and Cinquecento wished to, and did, write songs, but they wrote them in the same way that they would set a *Magnificat* or *Miserere*. And why? Because contrapuntal music was immeasurably stronger than any other, from the fact that it was a perfected and mature art; and when Corteccia and Festa and their contemporaries set themselves to write secular music they thought in the terms of choral composition.

Now choral and contrapuntal writing is a wonderful medium, capable of long intricate developments, grand climaxes and sustained effects. It can be terrifying, overwhelming or uplifting, but it was certainly unsuited to the interludes and dramatic performances. The day, moreover, was at hand when it would be ruthlessly thrown aside, and only twenty years after the death of Palestrina his music was barely heard outside Rome. It was driven out by the new method of figured bass, which quickly became the fashion, and, perhaps, by the desire for solo singing. The Italian audience, like the Italian singer, craved instinctively for *bel canto*, and at every opportunity, by the end of the sixteenth century, psalms, and, indeed, all Church music, was dressed up and disfigured in a mass of trills and runs and shakes.

There was certainly very little promise for the future in the musical plays of the Italian Courts, and yet from this very medley sprang the latest artistic product of the Renaissance in the form of the Opera. The outlook at the end of the Cinquecento was unfavourable enough, and to certain men among the audience of the Florentine pageants it seemed well-nigh hopeless. They were erudite scholars, music-loving gentlemen, grave and dignified, full of their own importance, burning with a passionate love of antiquity, and impressed with the great seriousness of art as they understood it. There was but little to attract and a great deal to repel such minds in the current performances at which they were invited to assist. Their reason was offended by the silliness of the play, their taste by the buffoonery and pretension of the acting and scenery. Was this, they asked, the level to which classical tragedy had sunk? They were disgusted at such a thought. Better no stage at all than one which only presented such a caricature of the gods and heroes of Greece and Rome. And so these refined, aristocratic dilettanti went home to ponder again over their precious manuscripts, but with a very distinct object in mind. The immediate result of their researches was to turn them from their learned occupations to the role of reformers. But they were quiet natures, and the reformation for which they strove was carried out by gentle and unobtrusive methods. The temperament of a Savonarola was completely lacking in them. One of their number, richer than the others, Giovanni Bardi, Conte di Vernio, made his house a centre where he gathered together his friends and many of the choicest spirits in Florence.

Casa Bardi was a typical old Florentine palace, with dark splendid rooms, and there, surrounded by beautiful things, Pietro Strozzi, Jacopo Corsi, Ottavio Rinuccini, Girolamo Mei, Jacopo Peri, Giulio Caccino, Andrea Salvadori, Marco di Gagliano, and Vincenzo Galilei, father of the great Galileo, met to discuss the arts and sciences. One subject, however, was nearest to all their hearts, and they had one artistic dream to which they aspired: how to improve, or, rather, create the music drama. True to their training, they looked backwards, not forwards, for a solution of their difficulties. The Greek theatre was to them the pattern of all perfection. Why not attempt to return to it? The Greeks had used music in their tragedies, though to what extent was not very clear, only a few bars from Euripides's *Orestes* having been preserved. No matter: if only, so they thought, the drama of antiquity could be revived, music would then regain its rightful place in dramatic art. Holding such views, it is hardly surprising that they looked with disgust at the inanity and showy emptiness of the interludes. To followers of Aristotle what could be more precious than unity? And of unity there was no trace in the Cinquecento stage, neither of time, place nor action, while every true Platonist revolted from this art of extravagant humbug.

The first move, therefore, must be to choose a theme, however simple, and carry it through without breaking the thread of dramatic interest. With this idea in mind, Vincenzo Galilei took the Count Ugolino episode from the *Divina Commedia*, and a passage from the Lamentations of Jeremiah, and set them, not as dramas, but more, as we should say, as cantatas. The great point was that he was striving for no outward effect, for nothing, in fact, but to provide simple declamatory music which should add to the meaning of the text.

This was, apparently, an unpretentious enough aspiration, but it brought Vincenzo at once into conflict with the whole school of contrapuntal tradition on the one hand, while, on the other, such work could be of little use in the functions and entertainments of the Court. From the outset, indeed, the Bardi circle seems to have realized that their conception of art differed widely from that of the masters of accomplished part-writing. Vincenzo, in his most interesting *Dialogo sopra la musica antica e moderna*, attacked Zarlino and the whole world of scholastic routine, on the ground that the formal intricacies and mannerisms of the contrapuntal school forbade all naturalness of expression.

He, perhaps not unnaturally, saw in contrapuntal art only a complicated maze, which jarred with all his own theories, and which he therefore condemned with cheerful and sincere one-sided thoroughness. Perhaps, in the main, he was right, when it came to evolving a style for dramatic declamation.

He brought forward some newly discovered fragments of Greek music in support of his arguments; but had he known it, there were other artists nearer at hand with whom also he would have been in sympathy. He had probably never heard of the Troubadours, and if he had, would almost surely have disapproved of them, and yet, as a matter of fact, he and they had the same artistic end in view. They both aimed at providing a fitting musical setting for poems, and eventually for larger works, and combining poetry and music in such a way that neither art should suffer. To us, *Count Ugolino* and the *Lamentations* seem harmless, bald, uninspiring compositions, certainly not such as to excite anyone; but the chosen public, who flocked to the Bardi Palace on the day of their first performance, was not only excited, it was thrilled. Here was a story illustrated without any of the external accessories to which people were accustomed, but which somehow they hardly missed: music which was so simple as to seem childish, and which yet was appropriate. They felt that Dante and Jeremiah were really speaking; and that at last the words were something more than just pegs on which to hang so much musical and scenic decoration. So this was what Count Giovanni and his friends had been planning, about which rumour had been busy. Well, it was new, it was interesting, it was worth the trouble of coming to hear; let them go on. Encouraged by this success, Galilei's friends determined on another and slightly bolder effort. Peri, Caccini, and Corsi took Rinuccini's fable of *Dafne*, which had the additional interest of action, and set it to music on the same lines as those Vincenzo had laid down. It was received with even more applause than the first venture, and, from having been a rather eccentric novelty, the Bardi circle suddenly found themselves growing famous with an enthusiastic following.

It became necessary to give this art a name: this treasure, which they so fondly believed they had been the first to discover, must not run the risk of confusion with any earlier or less enlightened form of music. Their style was to be what they called 'representative': poetry, emotion, dramatic action, were all to find enhanced expression in the music. It was to be the *Stile Rappresentativo*. Even the Court and the Grand Duke were interested. Peri, who from the beginning was in sympathy with the movement, was choirmaster to both Cosimo I and Cosimo II dei Medici, and, we may be sure, impressed upon his patrons how much their reputations as lovers of art would gain by being associated with so successful an enterprise. The Grand Duke was more than favourably inclined to Peri's arguments. The wedding of Maria dei Medici and Henri IV was approaching, and instead of only the usual confused performance, Peri should write the music for a drama in the new style for the occasion. The French ambassadors should see and hear how original and advanced music was at the Court of Florence. Peri justified all expectations. He took as his text Rinuccini's *Euridice*, and the choice was a happy one. The story lends itself admirably to music, and the guests who assembled in Palazzo Pitti on October 6th, 1600, at once felt the charm of *Euridice*. What is more, that charm still exists, and we who heard it two years ago in that same hall could well understand the enthusiasm of the Florentine Seicento public. Peri's aim was the same as Galilei's, and the mistake they, and all their friends, were making was in thinking they had invented the recitative (which existed to perfection in Plainsong), and in giving it a much greater importance than was due to it. Peri was not thinking of arias when he wrote in the preface to *Euridice:* 'In dramatic poetry, where it was necessary to imitate in singing the spoken language (for one never speaks in singing), I think that the ancient Greeks and Romans (who, according to general opinion, sang whole tragedies) used a musical tone (*un armonia*) which far surpassed ordinary speech and yet never developed into a sung melody, but remained an intermediary between the two.'

The success of *Euridice* was so great that the public at once demanded another play in the same style. This time it was Caccini's turn, and he set to work upon a new setting of Rinuccini's same *Euridice*, which was ready for the first performance on December 20th, 1600. He treated it with simple chords and progressions, but his songs, like the lovely Amarilli, show how much feeling and imagination he put into the simplest phrases.

His preface to *Euridice* is most interesting and shows how much was left to the skill of the performer in those early days of figured bass. He says: 'The harmony of the recitative is sustained by a *basso continuo*, and I have marked the most obvious chords of the fourth, sixth, seventh, and major and minor thirds, leaving the arrangement of the other parts to the judgement of the players. . . . In all my compositions I have never employed other art than the imitation of the sentiment expressed by the words, and I have used more or less tender notes as I judged might best impart that grace for which one searches in all good singing.'

Caccini was certainly one of the most genial composers of his day, and gifted with a great sense of beauty and musical good taste. He was born in Rome in 1550, but almost all his life was spent in Florence, where, as the popular 'Giulio Romano', he drew music-lovers to his house in Via Gino Capponi until his death in 1615. Caccini was an enthusiastic follower of Casa Bardi. In the preface to *Le Nuove Musiche* he says that he learnt more from the discussions which he heard there than in thirty years' study of counterpoint: 'Here I was advised to cultivate the art so highly praised by Plato and other philosophers, who affirmed that music is the orderly union of words, rhythm, and tone, if one desires that it should penetrate the hearer's intelligence and produce the wonderful effect admired by great writers, and which was impossible to obtain by counterpoint and modern methods. I understand that such music and musicians (Caccini is referring to the contrapuntal school) only give pleasure to the ear, since, owing to the lack of words, they could not speak to the spirit or stir its emotions. I therefore had the idea of introducing a musical form by which it should be possible to speak in music. To compose and sing well in this style a proper understanding of the idea and words is necessary, and taste in the reproduction of this idea by the use of the most expressive notes is far more useful than counterpoint, and I have only used the latter to hold together the different parts.'

What an interesting passage, written when the Roman school was at its height: written, what is more, without a shadow of doubt that only the *Stile Rappresentativo* was capable of stirring the emotions, or speaking to the spirit!

Caccini wrote a further drama, *Il Combattimento d' Apolline col Serpente*, on a poem of Bardi's, and a number of songs, and his idea of the aria was certainly more developed than that of Peri. His interest in singing was, perhaps, strengthened by the talent of his daughter Francesca, for whom, undoubtedly, many of his songs were written. He died in 1615, leaving her to add still further glory to the family.

She was not only celebrated as a singer, but was one of the best of all women composers, and wrote a number of madrigals, *ballate*, and dramatic works. She was sought after and admired as much as any *prima donna* of later years, and her fellow musicians of the opposite sex never seem to have grudged 'La Cecchina' her fame and popularity. She was the star of nearly all the Florentine festivities during the early

Seicento, and her compositions were constantly performed. She was the favourite of Society, and of the Grand Duke, and no Court entertainment was complete without her, while her husband and children apparently shared in her success. On several occasions she was associated with the poet Salvadori, and Marco da Gagliano, choirmaster of the Duke, who was attached to the Court, and composed a number of works in the, by now, all fashionable *Stile Rappresentativo*.

To Marco da Gagliano the music drama was everything, and he wrote of it: 'It is the true performance for princes, and more agreeable than any other, for it includes all the most noble pleasures. Imagination, form of subject and idea, style, the sweetness of poetry, the art of music, the concert of voices, and instruments, the art of singing, the lightness of the dances and movements, and one may say that painting also plays an important part in it by perspective, and dresses, whilst the intelligence and every noble sentiment is entirely charmed by the most agreeable arts ever invented by human genius.'

Marco da Gagliano, like many of his colleagues, was himself a singer, but he saw the danger in the ever increasing tendency to mere vocal virtuosity, and on this subject he utters words of wisdom: 'Many people fall into the error of endeavouring to introduce any number of trills, and runs and shakes, without any thought of the why or wherefore. Not that I intend to deprive myself of these ornaments, but where the drama does not call for them, let them be left on one side, in order not to be like some artists who, because they can paint cypresses successfully, put them into every corner of their pictures. On the contrary, the important thing is to pronounce the syllables clearly, that the words may be distinctly heard. That should be the continual aim of every singer, especially in the recitatives. Let him consider well that the pleasure of the listeners depends upon understanding the words.'

He wrote a *Daphne* and *Combattimento d' Apolline col Serpente*, for nearly all these composers chose the same familiar classical subjects. His stage injunctions about the dragon in the *Combattimento* seem very like those of only a few years ago regarding our friend the dragon in *Siegfried*. Marco says: 'The dragon should be large, and if the artist who designs it knows how to make it move its wings and spit fire (as I have myself seen), it will be most effective, but especially it must writhe and bend and, therefore, the man who works it must go on all-fours'!

The Bardi circle had certainly succeeded, one imagines, even beyond their own highest dreams. They had convinced their hearers that there was something, not only more artistic, but, all important point, more enjoyable, than the ordinary musical play and interludes.

In one respect, however, from their own point of view, they had failed signally, for in all these efforts they had certainly not attained to anything in the least like a revival of Greek tragedy. *Dafne* and *Euridice* have hardly the faintest resemblance to their Greek originals, as, indeed, how should they have? Were their creators disappointed at the difference, or were they too much occupied with their work even to notice it? None can tell, and most decidedly we are gainers by the fact that the theatre of Greece withheld its secrets, even from those who would have copied it most slavishly. For Galilei, Bardi, Rinuccini, Peri, and Caccini had not renewed a perfect thing of the past: they had made an imperfect thing of the present and future. They had actually laid the foundation of the modern opera and music drama, the one branch of musical art which has the mixed parentage of social necessity and intellectual reasoning. Unlike the greatest choral and instrumental music of the world, the opera, from its first beginnings until its highest development, was, and is, based upon compromise. A balance had to be struck between the claims of poetry, music, and staging, and the Bardi coterie had a firm hold of this truth. They knew that drama must represent human action, and that it could not, therefore, be overladen with a mass of extraneous matter, if it were still to keep its human interest. They dimly perceived that sincerity of expression was the first and all important consideration. Before going farther, let us hear from Pietro Bardi, the son of Conte Giovanni, what the *Stile Rappresentativo* meant for those most closely concerned with it. He is writing to his friend Giovanni Doni, and the letter runs:

'My father, the Signor Giovanni, had the greatest delight

in music, and besides being himself a composer of some merit, he always gathered around him all those men of the city who were most celebrated in the art. He invited them to his house and formed a most delectable "Accademia", free from all vice or gambling, where the noble youth of Florence was intellectually nourished. The time passed, not only with music, but also with lectures, discussions on poetry, astrology, and other sciences, all most profitable to such a society. At that time Vincenzo Galilei (father of the present great philosopher and mathematician) enjoyed vast renown, and he, receiving much pleasure from such worthy intercourse, sought to add to his masterly execution of music also a profound study of the theory of that art. In this purpose he was aided by other *virtuosi*, and spent many nights studying the Greek and Latin authors, together with our modern writers, so that in this way he became truly a master in the science of every branch of music.

'He saw that one of the chief objects of my father's circle was to revive, as far as possible, the music of the ancients, and from the available material, alas! so obscure, to attempt to improve our modern music, and to raise it from the miserable state in which it then was. He was, therefore, the first to bring forward songs in the *Stile Rappresentativo*, and being helped by my father, he took courage and passed long nights struggling along this stony path, jeered at by many, yet dedicating all his powers to this most worthy enterprise.

'The said Vincenzo showed every sign of gratitude to my

father, which he expressed most particularly in his book of ancient and modern music. He also composed the "Lament of Count Ugolino", by Dante, which was sung by a tenor of beautiful voice, accompanied by a body of violes of exquisite sound. This composition excited the envy of many professional musicians and *virtuosi*, and found favour with all true lovers of art. Galilei continued his noble undertaking and composed the Reproaches and Responses for Holy Week, which were sung in the presence of a most devout assembly. There was also at that time, in the circle of my father, a certain Giulio Caccini, young indeed in years, but esteemed a truly excellent singer of good taste. Finding himself drawn towards the new music, and receiving instructions from my father, he set various songs and other poems to music. These melodies were sung to the accompaniment of a single instrument, and were the delight of all who heard them.

'There was in Florence, in those days, also Jacopo Peri, the first pupil of Cristofano Malvezzi. He played the organ and other instruments, received the greatest praise for his compositions, and, as a singer, was highly esteemed by every one. Jacopo Peri, together with Giulio Caccini, gave himself up to following the *Stile Rappresentativo*, and avoiding a certain roughness and old-fashioned manner which was noticeable in the music of Galilei. They softened the new style until it moved the feelings of all who heard it. Thus, these two men acquired the reputation of having invented this new fashion of composition. Peri, with wide knowledge, having studied men's natural way of talking, which he could, moreover, wonderfully render in his music, while Giulio had the greater lightness of fancy in his compositions.

'A poem set to music by Peri in the *Stile Rappresentativo* was the fable *Dafne*, by the Signor Ottavio Rinuccini, which was performed privately in a small room, and whereat I, and many others, remained speechless with admiration. It was sung to the accompaniment of a body of instruments, and this arrangement was afterwards followed in other comedies. Great praise was given to Peri, Caccini, Signor Ottavio Rinuccini, and Jacopo Corsi, and many high and excellent ideas were given to the composers, which they subsequently carried out.

'After *Dafne* many fables were performed in the *Stile Rappresentativo,* all written by that excellent poet and master Signor Ottavio Rinuccini, together with his friend Corsi, who opened the hand of his liberality to the new art. These works were received with the utmost pleasure, *Euridice*, *Arianna* and many others being composed by the said Peri and Caccini. They found a number of imitators, both in Florence, the first home of their new music, and also in the other cities of Italy, and especially in Rome, where many marvellous plays were composed by different musicians, the best of whom would seem to be the now great Monteverde.

'I fear to have but poorly executed the command of your Excellency and Reverence to write to you on these matters, both by the tardiness of my service and meagre way I have performed it. There are now but few alive who remember the times of which I have written, but let my affection for those days persuade you of the truth of my judgement concerning them. Much might be said about the *Stile Rappresentativo*, and I have chosen but few instances in this letter, which I beg you to accept in the goodness of your heart.

'Thus I wish your Excellency and Reverence much happiness at this holy season of Christmas and I pray that Our Lord God will grant you all fruitful blessings.

'PIETRO BARDI

'*Florence, December* 16*th*, 1639.'

Pietro Bardi does not mention Emilio Cavaliere, a Roman who had been appointed Inspector of Fine Arts by the Grand Duke, and who died in Florence in 1602, and shared all Galilei's and Caccini's dislike of counterpoint. Did he influence the Bardi coterie, or the reverse? It is difficult to tell with any certainty. His name does not appear as though he had been an intimate of Casa Bardi and Casa Rinuccini, but his musical leaning was all away from contrapuntal and choral art, and towards a freer style of melody and accompaniment. His *Rappresentazione di anima e di corpo* was one of the first oratorios, and the publisher, Alessandro Guidotti (1600), advertises it with the announcement: 'We are here publishing some of the curious new musical compositions, written in imitation of the style which the ancient Greeks and Romans, it is said, employed in their theatres to provoke the most diverse passions in the souls of the spectators.'

Cavaliere wrote also at least three dramatic works: *Fileno*, *Satiro*, and *Il Giuoco alla Cieca*, and his stage directions are always very explicit. We learn that the orchestra was hidden behind curtains not to distract the audience, and that the chorus was about sixteen strong. 'It [the chorus] should sometimes sit, sometimes stand, endeavouring to listen to what is being performed and sometimes even should move about. When it has to sing it should stand, in order to facilitate dramatic gesture, and afterwards return to its place.'

With all their learning, our Florentine philosopher musicians played with their new toy with the pleasure of children, as well as with the seriousness of reformers!

The Bardi circle had done its work, and it remained for a more ardent and bolder nature than any of the Florentine composers to enshrine their principles in great musical dramatic compositions. This was the work of that startling genius, Claudio Monteverde. He was born in 1567, in Cremona, and was a pupil of an excellent composer of the Venetian school, Marco Ingegneri. Still quite young, we find him as singer, violinist, and choirmaster to the Court in Mantua, and a great favourite with the Duke, whom he accompanied on several journeys. In 1612 his master died, and Monteverde resigned his post, for more brilliant prospects were opening to him. His fame was already great, and the Venetians were determined to secure his services for Saint

Mark's. When his name was proposed no one else even stepped forward to compete for the appointment, and a higher salary was offered to him than to any of his predecessors. The *cappella* of Saint Mark's consisted of two organists, a choir-master, some thirty singers, and twenty-five instrumentalists, all picked musicians. The musical directorship of Saint Mark's was, after Saint Peter's in Rome, the best post in Italy, and it offered Monteverde an artistic *milieu* even more congenial than what he had found in Mantua. He never moved again, though he frequently composed works for other patrons and places, and he was the pride of the Venetians, who loaded him with honours. The government of the Republic was, indeed, ready to gratify his wishes in every way, sooner than face the possibility of some other city enticing him away from Venice. Quite late in life he became a priest and remained at Saint Mark's until his death in 1643. He was buried in the church of the Frari, but neither stone nor monument marks his grave, for which one looks in vain. In his younger days he had first become famous with some beautiful choral works, chiefly madrigals, and his first years in Venice were largely devoted to sacred music, which showed another side of his genius.

Already in his earlier compositions Monteverde's tendency was far in advance of his times. He hardly used the Plain-song modes, and his unexpected and bold modulations added enormously to the emotional power of his music. Is not the beautiful *Lamento di Arianna* one of the most expressive pieces of music? And one might quote many more of his arie. With Monteverde the recitative takes its proper place, and all due importance is given to it, but the aria has definitely come into its own. The beauty of the actual melody is sought after, and set in the chief place, from which it was never dethroned throughout all the subsequent history of Italian opera.

Even in the north of Italy there had been some attempts at dramatic composition, especially by Orazio Vecchi, the choirmaster and chief musician of Modena, born in 1550, whom Monteverde may well have known. His chief work was the *Anfiparnasso*, a *Commedia harmonica*, but it was still written in the old four-voice madrigal style, not with any idea of dramatic monody.

When the Duke of Mantua heard of the Florentine novelties, he at once wished for a similar drama for the theatre in Mantua, and Monteverde undertook to write it. This first attempt was brilliant. He took Striggio's poem of *Orfeo* and set it to music, with a power of emotional expression which is still fresh. No lapse of time hinders the effectiveness of Monteverde's inspiration, and his music is of that which never grows old. *Orfeo* was followed by *Arianna* and *La Finta pazza*, also written for Mantua, but one of the Venetian Senators, Mocenigo, anxious that the Venetians too should profit by their choirmaster's dramatic genius, arranged for performances in his own palace, now the Hotel Danieli, and *Il Combattimento di Tancredi e Clorinda*, and

Proserpina Rapita, on a text by Strozzi, were written for him.

In 1637 Venice opened its first opera house, and *Adone*, *Le nozze di Enea con Lavinia*, *Il Ritorno di Ulisse in patria*, and *L' Incoronazione di Poppea* were all performed there. Never before had such music been heard. The expressive arias moved the audience as nothing else could—those beautiful melodies which reflected so clearly the emotional situation—and we all know how lovely and touching Monteverde's phrases can be.

Monteverde was also the father of our modern instrumentation, and to him the different instruments in the orchestra were like people with their own individual character, each to be respected and allowed free play. He treated the instruments individually, or in families, and found many new effects, as, for instance, the tremolo of the strings in the *Combattimento*. He wrote with the unerring instinct of the born dramatic genius and great musician, and his instrumentation was as much a part of the drama as the words or vocal melody. For the first time the orchestra appears as an individual whole. It was unseen by the audience, and on this point Wagner was in agreement with all the early dramatic composers. Monteverde's orchestra consisted of two *gravicembali*, two *contrabassi da viola*, ten *viole da brazzo*, one *arpia doppia*, two *violini piccoli alla Francese*, two *chitarroni*, two *organi*, three *bassi da gamba*, one *regalo* (portable organ), four *tromboni*, two *cornetti*, one *flautino*, one *clarino*, three *trombe sordini.* Monteverde used all the resources and possibilities of instrumental music as he found it, and he carried it a long step farther and lifted it to a new level.

His success was enormous. In Bologna, Mantova, Parma, everywhere he triumphed. *Gloria del nostro secolo,* his contemporaries called him, doubtless feeling sure that the farthest limits of musical dramatic art had been reached. We may surely see in him the composer most typical of the age in which he lived, who more than any other carried the spirit of the Renaissance into the domain of musical art.

The Italian opera developed along quite other lines to those formulated by the Florentines and Monteverde, but Gluck repeated their theories, with all the added possibilities of the eighteenth century, and enriched the world with his unequalled pseudo-classical dramas. Wagner reaffirmed them in the language of the nineteenth century, and, as the result, we have *Meistersinger,* the *Nibelungen,* and *Tristan;* but the nursery of them all lies far away in the Bardi Palace in Florence, and Monteverde's study in Venice.

How much more might be said of these great musicians and this fascinating subject! But the origin of the music drama has been ably discussed in all its details, and Monteverde's and Palestrina's lives are well known to all music-lovers. This is but a bird's-eye view of Italian musical art, and, taking it as a whole, nothing is more striking than the length of time over which Italian creative musical power has extended. It began far away in the days of Saint Gregory, then flourished in the *Ars Nova* of the Trecento, and persisted triumphantly through the fifteenth and sixteenth centuries, creating new forms and developing new means. We see it continuing steadily through the Sei- and Settecento, and the influence of the schools of the great *virtuosi*, and of the *bel canto*, spread far and wide throughout Europe.

The passing Renaissance saw, it is true, the close of the most interesting phases of Florentine musical life. Gradually Florence became a provincial centre of mild intellectual bustle, but never anything else, and it was thus that Doctor Burney found it, whilst the greatest Tuscan composer of later years, Cherubini, was more at home in Paris than in Florence.

The other Italian cities, however, Rome, Venice, Naples, and Bologna, became celebrated for their musical societies and schools, and yielded the rich harvest of instrumental and vocal music throughout the seventeenth and eighteenth centuries. The period of baroque art was not that of baroque music, though the lightness and grace of many a Scarlatti or Corelli dance reflects all the charm of the rococo *salone* where it was first played.

We take leave of the musical Renaissance under the rising twin stars of the opera and oratorio, and looking towards the wide horizon of chamber and orchestral composition. The greatest music of the sixteenth century was in many ways alien from the spirit of the age which produced it, though it was in music that the Renaissance lived on, longer than in any other art. Pure choral music remained where Palestrina had left it, a light and beacon to succeeding generations; but the opening seventeenth century saw the development of many other ideas, the perfecting of other tentative experiments.

I have chosen to stop short at this particular point, not because there was any break in the musical tradition, but rather because the next period is already so well known.

This study, as I said at the beginning, is but an introduction, or an additional chapter to the great works on Renaissance art, an attempt to show a little of what the place of music was in Renaissance life. It is intended merely as a guide-book, whose only aim is here and there to open a door on some garden or courtyard which seemed to be shut; and do not we lovers of Italy all know the enchantment that so often lies behind the unpromising looking blank wall, or bolted *portone?* It is now for the traveller to push the door wide open, go in, and enjoy the many hidden beauties and delightful surprises which lie waiting for him throughout the course of Italian musical history.

LIST OF CHIEF COMPOSERS

FROM 1300 TO 1600

Franko	thirteenth century
Casella	thirteenth century
Walter Odington	*circa* 1260–1318
Garlandia	1290–*circa* 1340
Philippe de Vitry	1290–1361
Marchetto di Padova	late thirteenth–early fourteenth century
Joannes de Muris	early fourteenth century
Francesco Landino	1325–1390
Dunstable	1370–1453
Guillaume Dufay	1400–1474
Jean Okeghem	1430–1495
Antonio Squarcialupi	1436
Jakob Hobrecht	1450–1505
Arrigo Tedesco (Heinrich Isaak)	*circa* 1450–after 1519
Franchino Gafurio	1451–1522
Josquin de Près	*circa* 1460–early sixteenth century
Ottaviano Petrucci	1466–1539
Adrian Willaert	*circa* 1480
Johannes Tinctoris	1496–1511
Anton Brumel	late fifteenth century

List of Chief Composers from 1300 to 1600

Pierre La Rue	late fifteenth–early sixteenth century
Marchetto Cara	early sixteenth century
Alberto Ripa	sixteenth century
Annibale Padovano	sixteenth century
Deruta	sixteenth century
Matteo Rampollini	sixteenth century
Moschini	sixteenth century
Bartolomeo Tromboncino	sixteenth–seventeenth century
Andrea Gabrieli	1510–late sixteenth century
Nicola Vicentino	1511–1572
Cipriano da Rore	1516–1565
Gioseffo Zarlino	1517–1589
Giovanni Pierluigi (Palestrina)	*circa* 1524–1594
Orlando di Lasso	1532–1594
Vincenzo Galilei	1533–1600
Claudio Merulo	1533–1604
Alessandro Striggio	1535–
Costanzo Festa	† 1545
Gioseffo Guami	*circa* 1545
Marco Ingegneri	1545–1592
G. M. Nannini	1545–1607
Tommaso Vittoria	1546–1613
Francesco Suriano	1549–1620
Luca Marenzio	1550–1599
Emilio del Cavaliere	1550–1602

List of Chief Composers from 1300 to 1600

Orazio Vecchi	1550–1605
Giulio Caccini	1550–1618
G. B. Nannini	1550–1623
Giovanni Gabrieli	1557–1612
Felice Anerio	1560–1614
Jacopo Peri	1561–1633
Ludovico Viadana	1564–1627
Giovanni Continuo	1565
Adriano Banchieri	1565–1634
Claudio Monteverde	1567–1643
Giovanni Animuccia	†1570
Muzio Effren	*circa* 1570
Francesco Corteccia	1571
Antonio Cifra	1575–1638
Marco da Gagliano	1575–1642
Girolamo Frescobaldi	1583–1644
Gregorio Allegri	1584–1612
Paolo Agostini	1593–1629
Florenzio Maschera	late sixteenth century
Giovanni Valentini	late sixteenth–early seventeenth century
Francesca Caccini	late sixteenth–early seventeenth century
Luzzasco Luzzaschi	late sixteenth–early seventeenth century
Costanzo Porta	1601
Baldassare Donati	1603

BIBLIOGRAPHY

Ariosto, King of Court Poets	EDMUND GARDNER, *Constable,* 1906
Baldassare di Castiglione	JULIA CARTWRIGHT, *Murray,* 1908
Biographie Générale de la Musique	F. FÉTIS
Cantilene e Ballate. Strambotti e rispetti nei secoli XIII, XIV	GIOSUÉ CARDUCCI, *Pisa,* 1871
Cantilene e Ballate. Musica e Poesia nel mondo elegante Italiano del secolo XIV. Studii Letterarie	GIOSUÉ CARDUCCI, *Zanichelli. Bologna,* 1893
Compendio di cose nuove	VINCENZIO CALMETA, *Venice,* 1508
Cronaca di Firenze	GIOVANNI E MATTEO VILLANI, *Firenze,* 1825
Dante e i suoi tempi	ISIDORO DEL LUNGO, *Zanichelli,* 1888
Dictionary of Music and Musicians	SIR GEORGE GROVE
Dukes and Poets in Ferrara	EDMUND GARDNER, *Constable,* 1904

Bibliography

Florentia. Uomini e cose del Quattrocento	ISIDORO DEL LUNGO, *Florence,* 1897
Geschichte der Mensural Notation	JOHANNES WOLFF, *Leipzig,* 1904
Guillaume Dufay	C. VAN DEN BARREN, *Bruxelles. Hayez,* 1926
Histoire de l'Harmonie au Moyen Age	C. DE COUSSEMAKER, 1852
History of the Commonwealth of Florence	ADOLPHUS TROLLOPE, *Chapman & Hall,* 1865
Il Cortigiano	BALDASSARE CASTIGLIONE, *Sansoni,* 1916
Intorno alla Vita ed all' insegnamento di Vittorino da Feltre	CESARE GUASTI, *Firenze,* 1869
L'Art Harmonique au 12 et 13 siècles	C. DE COUSSEMAKER, 1865
L' Arte Musicale in Italia	LUIGI TORCHI, *Ricordi*
La Biblioteca Estense e la coltura Ferrarese ai tempi del Duca Ercole I	GIULIO BERTONI, *Turin,* 1903
La Poesia Popolare Italiana	A. D'ANCONA, *Livorno,* 1878
La Storia di Girolamo Savonarola	PASQUALE VILLARI, *Firenze. Le Monnier,* 1887

Bibliography

Ladies of the Italian Renaissance	CHRISTOPHER HARE, *Harper,* 1907
Le Origini del Teatro Italiano	A. D'ANCONA, *Turin,* 1891
Le Stanze, l' Orfeo e le rime	ANGIOLO POLIZIANO, *Firenze. Bardera,* 1868
Les Femmes de la Renaissance	DE MAULDE CLAVIÈRE, *Perrin et Cie,* 1904
Libro Primo di Laudi spirituali	FRA SERAFINO RAZZI, *Venice,* 1563
Libro delle Laudi	G. ANIMUCCIA, *Roma,* 1570
Libro di Laudi spirituali	Printed for the Rev. Fathers of the Oratory in Rome by A. GARDANO, 1589
Libro di Madrigali	ARCADELT, *Venice,* 1539
Life of Isabella d' Este	JULIA CARTWRIGHT, *John Murray,* 1904
Life of Beatrice d' Este	JULIA CARTWRIGHT, *Dent,* 1905
Lirica Antica, thirteenth, fourteenth, fifteenth centuries	EUGENIA LEVI, *Bemporad,* 1908
Lirica Antica, sixteenth, seventeenth centuries	EUGENIA LEVI, *Olschi,* 1909

Bibliography

Lives of the Early Medici	JANET ROSS, *Chatto & Windus*, 1910
Mantova e Urbino	A. LUZIO E. R. RENIER, *Torino. Roux*, 1893
Memoirs of the Dukes of Urbino	JAMES DENNISTOUN, *John Lane*, 1919
Men and Manners of Old Florence	GUIDO BIAGI, *Fisher Unwin*, 1919
Musik Lexikon	HUGO RIEMANN, *Leipzig*, 1900
Musique Ancienne	WANDA LANDOWSKA, *Paris*, 1921
Palestrina	MICHEL BRENET, *Paris*, 1906
Poesie Italiane Inedite	FRANCESCO TRUCCHI, *Guasti*, 1847
Poesie di Lorenzo il Magnifico	G. CARDUCCI, *Firenze*, 1859
Poesie Musicali dei secoli XIV, XV, XVI	ANTONIO CAPPELLI, *Bologna*, 1868
Primo Libro d' arie musicali	G. FRESCOBALDI, *Firenze*, 1630
Primo Libro di Madrigali	A. STRIGGIO, *Venice*, 1560
Primo Libro di Musiche	F. CACCINI, *Firenze*, 1618

Bibliography

Scherzi Musicali a 3 voci	C. MONTEVERDE, *Venice*, 1609
Storia d' Italia	GUICCIARDINI, *Pisa*, 1819
Storia d' Italia	F. GUICCIARDINI, *Turin*, 1874
The Civilization of the Renaissance of Italy	JAKOB BURCKHARDT, *Sonnenschein*, 1904. *English translation by Middlemore*
The Evolution of the Art of Music	SIR HUBERT PARRY, *Kegan Paul*, 1905
The Renaissance	WALTER PATER, *Macmillan*, 1917
The Renaissance in Italy	J. A. SYMONDS, *Smith, Elder*, 1898
Vite di Uomini illustri del secolo XV	VESPASIANO DI BISTICCI, *Ludovico Frati. Bologna*, 1892
Vittorino da Feltre	WILLIAM H. WOODWARD, *Cambridge*, 1905